SENSE OF MEMORY

SENSE OF MEMORY

DIARY OF A BITTER HEART

Catherine Vi Tran

Writers Club Press

San Jose   New York   Lincoln   Shanghai

SENSE OF MEMORY
DIARY OF A BITTER HEART

Writers Club Press
an imprint of iUniverse, Inc.

For information address:
iUniverse, Inc.
5220 S. 16th St., Suite 200
Lincoln, NE 68512
www.iuniverse.com

ISBN: 0-595-20419-8

Printed in the United States of America

Foreword

Thank you to my parent who supported my thoughts in this fiction. to my dearest and loveliest sister who always enlightened me, "Choose one thing and go for it until the end. Don't be distracted, okay!". To my soulful boyfriend who always encouraged me to write this book, "Many complication had happenned unexpectedly within your life. Now it's time to express them". Most important words of all, thank you to all my readers, without you my past forever will be hidden in pain. To write this book I depended on the indulgence, livelihood, advices, forethought of my sister, my boyfriend, my life experiences, and many sources of researches.

Preface

To the people
who taugh me more than I know.
This drama is based on a true story.

Approach

Save golds for the descendants,
the descendants will possibly waste all.
Save books for the descendants,
The descendants may not read the books.
In spite of that,
Save virtual scarlet past,
The descendants can always perceive the knowledge,
and the wisdom from the knowledge.

Introduction

Each time the tamarind leaves fell; they fell like rain. Tamarind leaves scattering fell each time the wind softly passed by. Until the old tree leaves had fell off, there were only branches of twigs remained. It was not for long for the new tamarind buds grew back. Then, the tamarind buds became the baby green leaves. The tamarind leaves grew like students were changing clothes. Now, perhaps, the convent where I used to study there was covered with green tamarind leaves. Why I never had a chance to come back the convent, walking through the falling tamarind leaves? Each of the tamarind leaves was a drop of my tear. The convent was still there in my memory, but in my dream I heard the tamarind leaves wishpered to me, "Life is bitter and that's the way it is. It's just like tamarind leaves always sour while other leaves are sweet. If there is no Lily in this world, who will endure the pain. Where will sour go if sweetness is all over the place?" I was born in a tearful family and my parent left me for my maternal grandma to take care of when I was a one-year-old baby. Peace of the Communist didn't bring me any luck but a cruel life beside my maternal grandma. My dad left Vietnam when I was a one-year-old baby because he couldn't live under the Communist's ruling. My mom remarried and experienced a cracking life with her three little children, but her life was still lonely and never had the word "Peace" in her mind. I lived in a neighborhood where there was many tragics. Almost the children I knew, they also didn't have fathers. Some of them their fathers died in the war. Some of them, their fathers were in the concentration camp. Some of them, their fathers escaped to another foreign countries. There were some lucky had fathers but those men often absenced from homes. When they went homes, they became grouchy and beated their children like they wanted to put all their angers on their innocent children to release their depression. I wished those happy fairy tales that my maternal grandpa told me since of was three or four years old coming true someday. If there was fairy lady giving me three wishes. The first wish I would wish I have a trustful father; the second wish I would wish my mom has back a normal life; and the third wish I would wish I have enough confidence in myself to wear a white long dress going under falling green tamarind leaves or I would wish desolation children in this world could have a normal life. Who would give those simple wishes like that? I understand why those sour tamarind leaves never could speak.

Life in Vietnam

There is a time in the life of every problem when it is big enough to see,
yet small enough to solve.
Mike Leavitt.

Happy families are alike.
Every unhappy family is unhappy in its own way.
Leo Tolstoy

In time of test, family is best.
Saying

01

I lived in a medium and prosperous family near the heart of Saigon before the Vietnamese war and during my maternal grandpa was still alive. Saigon in my eyes was big like the whole world because I never went anywhere else outside Vietnam, not until I was sixteen. Even though I lived in Saigon, a capital city in the South of Vietnam, but I had never seen Hanoi, a capital city in the North of Vietnam where my parents were born. I did not know Vietnam was divived into three regions: North, Middle, and South. I knew nothing about the outside world until one day. I started to asked myself, "Where was my father? why he was not with me?"

My mom and I faced a new life without my father. After the Vietnamese war in 1975, the Communist started to govern Vietnam. I never unsterstood the word "Communist". Mom and I lived with my maternal grandparent, my aunts, and my uncles in a three-story house that faced directly to the main street of Saigon. Each story of the house had three bedrooms and one living room. On each story, the bedroom that connected to the balcony facing directly to the front street but it was without bathroom. Two other bedrooms on the back of the story were without balconies attaching, but they had bathrooms in them. Those bedrooms on the back didn't face to the front street. I didn't remember how many bedrooms and bathrooms we had all together but I had seven aunts and two uncles. At the time I was living in that house, four out of seven aunts were married included my mom. I didn't know what the word

"Marry" to all my aunts, but I had rarely seen those husbands of my aunts. The men had to work for their living survival and as a teenager I didn't understand anything but seeing all my marrying aunts and my mom were lonely and broken heart with their desperated children. Each family reserved a room, and all the single women lived together in one room accepted single men. Each of my uncle got a room of their own because I got only two uncles. I only saw three men in the house that were my grandpa and two of my uncles. No wonder my grandma spoilled those uncles of mine to extreme. I never complained for anything. In fact, I felt I was lucky than many of children wandered on the street begging for foods and find themselves shelter everyday. Somehow, I felt half of my heart was somewhere else searching for an unsolved question.

The main street was always busy with many kinds of transportation traveling around the city everyday. The street was always crowded and filled with noise. The noises from the vehicles traveled around, the street sellers roamed for their delicious snacks, and the bargained voices from the street shops were so used to my ears. Those noises were not the problems. In fact, if any day I did not hear those noises I would be very surprised and assumed there must be problems. It was true that there was a little Amerasian boy about seven years old selling Vietnamese rice waffers near my house. Everyday he passed by my house roaming to advertise his waffers. Once, I didn't hear his voice any longer and asked his mom where he was when I accidentally saw her on my way to school. I was downhearted and sorry to hear that his own mother sold him for $800 U.S dollars to another family because she found out he got sick. People used the boy to go to America. Before the war, many American soldiers had affair with Vietnamese women. After the war was over, the United States was getting those Amerasian back and allowed the family who took care of them going along too. That was why people who wanted to go to American just get themselves an Amerasian so they could go along. I did not know what to say to the boy's mother. I asked myself "Did she have a heart?" or the situation was so bitter that she could not affort to feed a child? I could not imagine my mom selling me as an object during my sickness. What about the boy could not be sold and disabled? His mother could have leaving him on the street and running without any tears. She sold her son anyway and said it was a shame for her to keep the boy because the boy reminded her past as a pitch. I didn't think that was a good excuse for her to sell her own delivery son. What kind of mother was that? She was a devil that her action could not be forgave. I was beside that boy corpse eight months after he was sold to another family. He died for some dieases that I quite didn't know but I was so surprised that his mom and the family who bought him were argued with each other beside his corpse without being any concern about the poor death boy. The other family wanted the money back, and the boy's mother said when it was sold it could not be returned. They didn't have the humanity in them. They threw the boy corpse in the trash without proper burrial for he was useless to them. I didn't know that I missed the roaming voice of the seven years old boy or he told me in my dream that he was free from his dispirited society. This was a human being who I thought was treated worser than an object.

One of my uncle taugh me how to ride bicycle when I was ten years old. The bicycle was the most important transportation that helped me traveling around the city at that time. My mom used to drive me or I used to walked to school everyday since I was fifth grade. I remembered the first time I was ever driving on my new bike that my mom bought for me when I was ten years old. I drove around the places of the city without being tired. As a ten-year-old girl, I felt I had all the freedom in the world, but my thought was not what I imagined. It was just a fantasy dream in a mind of an innocent girl. It was just a moment of excitement when a girl had her new toy, a bike. I did not know this big world had more tragic than just the voice of the seven-year-old boy got throwing into the trash when died of being useless to his mother. My bike got stolent by some thieves that attacked in my house ten days after I got the bike. I was crying not because I lost the bike, but I felt sorry and pity for my mom because she worked so hard for many years despite of sickness in order to buy the bike for me. What made me growing so fast? Becoming a mature girl each day was what people said to me. I lost my purity at the age of twelve. The purity was the inborn beauty that I never had, but I realized that to become a mature girl, I had to pay a price. The price that worthed my life because nothing in this life was free. What did I mean by purity? When I was twelve, I used to wash clothes for my family each morning. My grandma let another family rented the front region of the house to sell noodle soup every morning. A bastard man, who was the husband of the noodle selling lady, molested me. Every time he saw me came down washing clothes, he tried to sit behind my back, wrapped his hands around my breasts, and rubbed vigorously that made my breasts so hurtful. I used to cried and yelled for help, but no one had seem to hear my utterance. I told him letting me alone, but he didn't want to yield and he was hundred times stronger than I did. I wanted to tell his wife so bad, but thinking about two of his daughter (two of his daughters were my friends) I stopped telling because I didn't want to break up his family. His children wanted their parent as much as I wanted my parent. I knew how painful and suffer it was of not having parent around me. Since I was seven year old, seeing the entire high school students wore the beautiful long white dress, I always wished that one day it will be my time to wear the long white dress like those students. I remembered my grandpa often sang to me a lovely song name, "The Age of Purity". It remarked, "Please, give me the white long silk dress perfumed the purity and soft like the clouds, I will wear it to greet my parent on the coming new year day and go to school with books on my bike meeting my new friends and teachers. I can feel my silky long white dress worthed more than the age of purity." I silently cried whenever remembered that song grandpa sang to me. I felt dirt and shame covering all over my body. The white long dress wasn't for me anymore. I exchanged it for something that had seemed destroying my whole life. I sacrificed my purity to keep peace in their family, but did they think of me? My half-sister usually said, "The harm that you put in others, you would receive that harm back in the future." That man put harm into me, but I hadn't seen any harm coming to him. I hid that secret inside and thought I had to endure the pain forever. Today, my half-sister and I walked on the same way; she saw my pain through the conversation between us and said, "I understand why your heart is bleeding and no bandage can absorb that heavy stream of blood inside of you." I had seen nothing harm to that molested man so far. In American, they didn't expect a high school girl to wear a white long dress. They encouraged a foreigner to keep their custom, but that was not required. Many Vietnamese girls felt proud to wear the white long dresses, but I only wore the white long dress when I felt heartless and sorry in myself.

I grew up during the the time the Communist ruled Vietnam. People lived in fear for money changing value almost everyday. The government did not care how much a family had, all the old printed types of money must threw away. They gave each family the new printed types of money in a limited amount. My grandma scolded bitterly, "The hell stole from us one million and gave us back just a hundred thousand (Vietnamese monetary). The godless and cutthroat Communist". I was too little to understand about the Communist. All the actions that I had witnessed through my own eyes were since the Communist took over; my family did not have enough money for living survival. We had to mix sweet potatoes with rice to eat because sweet potatoes were cheaper than rice in Vietnam. Eating the combination of rices and sweet potatoes was the only way we could save money for the rainy day. I remembered I was always picking the sweet potatoes to eat first, and my tears were dropped along with the tiny portion of rice left over after picking out all the sweet potatoes. There were almost twenty people in the family and only one of the member was working to feed twenty of them. My maternal grandpa was the only one person who was working to feed the whole family of twenty. All the members in the family were unemployed after my maternal grandpa left the house and I was too young to remember exactly the year we experienced all the tragic. Money lost its value increasingly each day; my maternal grandma saved golds instead of money because gold seldom changed its value. Saving golds became a tradition; although most of Vietnamese were living in America, they still had the fear that famine would come to them any time.

One day, several men from the government came to my house in Vietnam, took away the furniture, and burned them. The flame mingled with our compressing anger. They said we brought the furniture in the period of the American was in Vietnam. Anyone in the family who worked for the American and inherited the American benefit would be considered betraying the country (My grandpa worked as an accountant for the 3M Company before the Vietnamese war). The Communist burned all the furniture without caring that we did not have any left to use or any money to buy the new one. All the family's members were angry, but all we could do were compressed our anger or else we could be executed for against the laws of the communist. At that time, everyone started to pay attention to those futons that filled with dusts in the garage for years. I did not know what to think but listened to all my grandma whinning words all day. Grandma had her point that the war was over; furniture was just object. Furniture was not there to kill the government. Burning the furniture did not make the government getting any better. However, the citizens would become more bias to the government for destroying worthy properties and wasting money that affected badly to the economic. If my grandpa was wrong for being an American worker, they should punish my grandpa not the furniture. The furniture was faultless. we felt so ashame and helpless to said that. we could not even protect an object belong to ourselves.

Whenever the situation of the burning furniture was reminded, a very valuable story my maternal grandpa used to tell me about a king and his servant. There was a king who had a precious horse and gave to one of his servants to take good care of it. Unfortunately, the horse suddenly died. The king was so angry and magligned that the servant had killed the horse. The king wanted to prosecute the servant, but one of the king's officers stopped the king. The officer said, "This convicted felon earned a death penalty without knowing his fault. Then, people still assumed he was innocent. If we explained for him why he earned his death, he would die in peace and we made ourselves proficient to the citizens." The king agreed to the officer and called the soldiers taking the servant out to hear his verdict. The officer pronounced to the servant, who was a criminal making the horse died, "You had three sins worth death penalty. First sin, you were not taking good care of the king's horse. Second sin, you let the most precious horse that the king loved more than his own life died. Last sin, you made the king notorious to the citizens that only the horse, the king's anger had killed a human life. The citizens in the country when heard would feel repulsion toward the king. Other foreign countries would hold the king's contempt. You made everything disharmony only because of a horse. That was why you deserved to died." Then, the officer called to lock up the servant again waiting for the final verdict from the king. After hearing the officer's verdict, the king felt regretful. He called, "Please, release the servant. I don't want to be a benevolent."

I wished the Communist would feel like the king. They should realize their vengeance and anger had destroyed the innocent people without justice and humanity. If the Communist realized their fault like the king, my family would have not been through many tragic. One of my aunts married at the age of eighteen and went to the United States with her husband. I felt sorry for my aunt. She said she did not have any feeling or passion for her husband for the first five years living together. She had done all the responsibilities of a mother perfectly. Even though she was married, we still needed her and relied on her. She was the only one that we put all hope on and I was so lucky to have a helpful aunt in this world. However, I didn't know what to blame on; my aunt's generousity was paid back by a sadful family. Her husband was having an affair with another woman. Her daughter was pregnant without knowing who was the real father. Sadness was all around my aunt, but she hid it to keep her family go on so she could at least complete her responsibility to help her daughter. That was where the heart is.

Since the Communist took over, my maternal grandpa tried to escape from the Communist. From the escaping day, no one heard about him any longer; either he was death or alive somewhere during his trip no one knew. Grandpa knew the escaping trip would be deadly, but he still risked himself to death just to get away from the Communist. He rather died than lived under the Communist's rules. After 1975, the Communist put all the Vietnamese soldiers, who served in the armed forces before 1975, in prison. The higher rank a solder served in the Army, the more years he had to spend in prison. I knew one of an excellent math teacher named Al. He was mute after fifteen years he had put in jail by the Communist because of working for the CIA. His children had no idea why they could not get any help in math during they were in school. Al just sat silently at home all day. One day one of his children got home from school saying to his wife, "Mom, does this man really my dad? He is useless and retarded. I got an A in my math test without any help from him and he is a math teacher." In the next day, Al killed himself by taking rat's poisoning. His son told me, "If I knew my words were that effective I could have said that sooner. I didn't want my dad to suffer. His brain was seriously damaged after the bloody war." I didn't know what to say. May be the son was so cruel, but he also had his point. Most of the prisoners were cracked and mentally ill. I didn't know much about politic. After all, I saw Vietnamese was against Vietnamese. The mother country endured the pain, desperation, lost, and under-development, could not go up, forever poor, and hungry. I felt sorry for myself when talked about what I witnessed about my country and could not do anything to help. It was scary when I heard the word "Death". Death was ended, but my maternal grandpa still tried the trial of death. Grandpa thought he was born to be death. Not yet one of my pretty aunt also tried to escape to American too. She went by boat and I was so scare when she told me all the events during her escaping trip. Of course she had to hide from the Communist for days until the sea was calm. While her friends, her husband, and she were on the sea trying to find the way, the pirates were attacked them. The pirates wanted all the women to get on their boat. My aunt's husband told her to hide under a box and he poured all the black oil all over her. The pirates took all the women accepted my aunt. May be she was so dirty that they found her useless. So they returned her and raped all others women. Some of the women were died in the beginning right after they got raped . Some of them survived, but they were losing their strenght and seriously sick until death. My aunt was a lucky one, but she was terrified. She recovered after a while when one of foreign boat took her to Galang island, a place where they helped the survivors and my aunt was one of the suffocated survivors. Morever, one of my neigbors escaped with two of his sons. They were hungry during the trip and one of his son died. My neighbor and the other son had to eat the flesh from the death human body. When the son ate his own bother flesh, his skin was getting yellow and got ill after he got survived on the island; he got weaker each day and died anyway during living on the island. The father was healthier than his son; he made it through to America, but he got crazy and suffering each day for his mind always reminded him about his sons; he died for being so frightened and destroyed himself. As a ten years old girl, I thought of how brave the Vietnamese people were; they decided when they knew they would be died any time on their escaping trip to America. When my supportive aunt was not married yet, my maternal grandpa was the only source of financial support for the whole family of twenty. Since he had gone, the whole family had to depened on my aunt in the United States for living survival. It was hard to find a job in Vietnam, especially women. We did-n't do any business or anything. I had seven aunts. Since my maternal grandpa had gone on the trip to America and disappeared forever after his departed. Every months my aunt in America had to send money helping the family in Vietnam. If she sent money late on any month, we had to eat foods sparingly each day. My maternal grandma controlled all the money. A lot of times, one pound of pork meat could provide for the whole fam-ily of twenty people. All my aunts started to worked so hard to support themselves, but it seemed never enough to survive. They went to the countryside where my maternal grandpa's sister lived there, to open a coffee shop. They used their natural beauty to work as the waitresses in the coffee shop. Men came for their beauties and then their coffee. It was pathetic and pitiful. What could they do? At least, they were just waitresses not those pitches sleeping around with hungry men.

A typical doctor in Vietnam earned about a hundred dollars a month. People could not afford to be sick. My mom worked in a black market near home. She earned twice as much as the doctor. In fact, she knew many doctors, but that was how her life became miserable and suffer. The doctors usually prescribed and prefered the patient to buy medications from my mom. My mom was not a pharmacist, but she knew many kind of medications. In America, only a graduated pharmacist could sell the prescribed medications. However, in Vietnam people did anything for living survival. Once I was at a drug store and saw many customers came in buying medications. They did not have doctors' prescriptions. One of the women came in and said, "I have heartburn and nervous breakdown." The seller gave the woman a bag which enclosed several kinds of medications and said, "Twenty thousand, please." (This was about one dollar and fifty cents in U.S Dollar). I wondered why the customer who bought the medications did not care about either the medications were right for her or not for her. All she knew were she could afford the medications for her sickness. There was no pharmacist in the selling medication shop either. One of my aunt brought me some medications when I had fever. The medications had different colors but no instruction or seal boxes for them. I asked my aunt to make sure I had the right medications. She gave me the box, but the instruction on the box was written in French and she knew nothing about French. She said she regconized and memorized the medications by colors when the drug seller sold to her. I suspected that what about the drug seller? Did he/she know how dangerous it was to sell the drugs without any prescriptions and he/she was instructed people taking the medications without pharmacist's lisence. People did not sue each other like in America. They had no money to buy insurance to protect themselves in danger. They could not afford to feed themselves two major meals each day to survive, how could they pay to protect their healthcare. If they could pay for the insurance, could the insurance company be reliable or responsible enough for the clients. Living in this corrupted society, either the insurance company took all the money and ran away or the clients arranged many ways to get the great deal of money from the insurance. The poor was getting poorer each day and the rich was getting richer each day. I asked my mom, "why?" and her answer was a question, "Why god gave birth to the elephants and the grasses under their feet? God must have his purpose. If there were only doctors in this world, who would be patients? If there was no patient, who would buy your mom medications?" My mom knew that she had been doing a wrong job, but who would feed her children. To be a responsible mother, she had to do the illegal work. If she could cry all day in order to help her children to survive, she would volunteer to do that. My mom had no more tear but faced the tragic for her children. I was too young to think of a dysfunctional family and a corrupted society in Vietnam. What I saw sometimes was pitiful and painful. That was how the tamarind leaves were always sour.

Depression

Depression…is caused by loss of hope.
John Leifer

Life is too short to be little.
Disraeli

02

The world is a gigantic school. Desperation is an excellent instructor, and self-consciousness is a bestfriend who helps its friend to be a decent human being. Sometime, people asked me, "Who do you look like?" I just smiled, but never answered. I think most of people got themselves an answer, "She is a replication of her dad." after they looked at my mom comparing to me. What was special about the appearance? It was not a pleasure for me to hear that I am a replication of my dad. It was not because I hated him. In fact, I would be flatter and proud for whom I looked like if my maternal grandma treated me nicely and respectably despite of my ugly look. My grandma used to say to me, "You have an oval face just like your dad; a girl considerred unlucky with oval face shape. Your nose is big like a dragon head. Your nose's shape make your face dull, lack of keenness, and big nose is a sign of losing money. Your eyes are long like evil snake. I feel sorry for me to keep a hell like you." As a twelve years old girl, I felt offensive whenever I heard grandma's insulting voice speci-fied my ugliness; even though it was the truth, she should not say that to a little girl. I was a very sensitive girl and took her words seriously. She was never cared how I felt because she thought I was just a little innocent girl under her control. As I grew up with my maternal grandparent, I got used to grandma's words because she was a cruel grandma who perhaps did not know what she was doing and talking about. However, some other of my relatives, they also loved and complimented my pretty cousins more than me. I was not jealous because they weren't paid any attention to me, but because they treated me like shit. I was lonely and felt so bad as a little girl when they told how ugly I was compared to some of my cousins. I was the one always did the most works like washing dishes, helping to prepare the foods, set up the tables, and cleaned up everything while some others pretty cousins of mine just sit around hearing compliments about them. The older people didn't care about how hard I worked to prepare for the party, they felt the appearance was more useful than my hard works. I did-n't give a dam for what they said about my ugliness because they always hurted me that way anyhow. However, I expected at least they gave me some help for the party. Luckily I had a strenght to handle the works or else I could have died without anybody care. Once, one of my cousins and I were argued about she didn't help me anything to prepare the party. She told me that was my job to do because I was ugly and didn't attract people to love me. In that way, I didn't entertain people and they found me bor-ing. She said beauty often was a great topic for people to gossip, but ugli-ness was never an interested one. I was so angry after what my cousin told me. I ran to her and was about to spit on her face to release my anger. Unfortunately, her father came stopping me and said, "Why don't you set-tle in silence while you still depended on other people. It was a big mistake for you to have war with my daughter. Back off and do your own work." He held his daughter on his arm trying to protect her and said sorry to her without trying to know who fault was that. The action of my cousin's father reminded me a short story about a rich man which I used to hear from my grandpa. Once, there was a storm and his wall protecting the house was broken down. His son told him, "If you not build the wall right away, thief will attrach our house". The neighbor also told the rich man the same thing like his son told. The wall was waiting to be built in the morning, but that nigh the thief came roping his house. The rich man complimented his son that his son was smart predicting the right thing, but the rich man blamed on the neighbor suspecting that the neighbor was the thief. I learned that I had to be careful before proceding any action. People in the same house usually protected their blood than stranger. I had to make statement to the right people or else I will get into trouble and waste my time for being concern to them. My cousin's father believed his daughter than me. It seemed like he intentionally injured me because he didn't want to figure out who was right and wrong. I always cried by myself for the maltreating that people behaved to me. Why? because I was hideous? I thought they were hideous than me because they didn't have a loving heart for a lonely girl without father.

If I had to describe myself into words, I would say my look is average. I had a slim 5'5" tall body. My skin is a combination of white-yellow Asian, but a little bit hairy. The appearance was not a principal subject that I wanted to discuss here. My appearance had nothing to do with my personality and characteristic at all although my name was well matched with my face. I would give up if anyone wanted to compare me with another person's beauty; even though the person's beauty is under average. All those compliments from the people about my look, whether they were good or bad, I really did not give a dam because I would think they were all liers anyhow. My mom called me Lily because she said the flower was rare by the time I was born. My body was slim and my life was rare like Lily flower. That was what my mom said to me. My mom was right Lily was my favorite flower.

I was born in Saigon, one of the Capital cities in the South of Vietnam, and cried with many other babies were not as bad as my life turned out to be. Saigon, a capital city in the south of Vietnam where I was born, had been through many obstacles for many years in my eyes. The Vietnamese war brought many tragic to people, and one of the painful tragic was families' separation. Many women waited for their husbands to release from the war, but most of the soldiers died during the war or went home with both physical and mental wounds. A woman, all by herself worked so hard to feed her disable husband and innocent children. How could I hold my tears for all the desperation that Vietnam, my motherland, had endure from the war? The Vietnamese people were still under control of the

Communist. The people were still in fear after the war and still tried to escape from the Communist each day. My wound was not a serious injury as many other soldiers received from the war. One of my suffering wounds was caused by family's separation. The separation was the pain in my heart. The memory of sorrow caused by my maternal grandma, the relationship that turned into a hurtful reality, and the people that totally influented my character.

One of my Vietnamese poets, Vu Hoi, had expressed his discouraging feeling in a poem. The poem revealed his boredom when everything in his life was not completed as the way it seemed to be. Vu Hoi felt pity for his life. In Vietnam, writing poems was not an encouraging field. Although his written poem was an excellent work of art, most of people did not have time to appreciate or to enjoy the inspiration of the poems. It was not because people didn't like him or didn't want to appreciate. It was because their works for living survival could not depend on the poems. They could not eat poems to survive or to do business with the poems. In fact, poems were the unreality works that most people tried to avoid. Vu hoi's poems were the delight works. One of his poems that attracted me, "Half and Half" expressed his feeling of being in the middle of the road and headed to nowhere in life. The poem had translated into English version as follow:

Life is a combination of a half-of- awakening and a half-of-drinking.

A half-of-black, a half-of-white, a half-of-day light, and a half-of-night.

A mix feeling of a half-of-happiness with a half-of-sadness.

A half-of-river sand-bank and a half-slope-of-mountain high.

A half-of-love and a half-of-missing the suffocated tears.

A half-of-earnestly smile and a half-of-disappointed love.

A half-of-the soul under the eyes-of- short life.

Unstable in a half-of-an itinerary ups and downs life.

Flickering in a half-of-uneasy sleep, late in the night.

Bitterly laugh beside the oil lamp in the middle of the night.

My sister ususally whinned at me for living in an unreality world of poems, but she never stopped me for loving poems and it was my hobby. I loved poems because I could feel clearly the touch of poem as I felt Vu Hoi's feeling. My life was an incompleted. Poems garnished theirs beauties upon my life and gave me a sense of hope for a better life. Poems transformed my dual life into a soften soul. All human beings had hopes, dreams, sorrows, and curiosities in their life. The above favorite poem revealed the secret of the soul. The sentimental soul had concealed many of memories.

Faith was not what I believed in. I am a catholic and my belief is strongly in Jesus Chris. Jesus is my highest god whom my ancestor had worshipped and passed on through many generations. I also respected other religious as long as a religious taught me kindness, loveliness, respectiveness, and humanities. Believing in other religious did not mean I was betraying my Catholic religious or weakening my belief in Jesus. God created me and gave me a soul to face the hardship of life. I suffered through many difficult situations with a tentative assumption that I learned from grandpa, never give up hope in myself and there will never be the end of the world. Sadness turned me into a strong person, but also a sentimental individual as well. I did not know who should be blamed for turning my life into a lunatic or that the way life should be for me. Many times, I hated myself for not forgiving others, but how could I forget all those memories that had affect my life so badly. I also loved philosophy and my most respectable chinese philosopher was Confucius. He gathered group of intelligent disciples whom he trained in literature, music, human relations, and ethics; taught that rulers exist to secure happiness of subjects, that family provides model for all human relations. I learned many valueable stories from him, but still I was a type of person who taking everything seriouly. I only forgive other when I could forgive myself.

In Vietnam, no one ever told me why my family separated and I never asked about the separation until I was old enough to understand. I always thought because my mom was remarried that why my dad left. The mother usually had to keep the child and I was with mom. My aunts usually told me that my parents destined to meet each other but faith did not arrange them to live in a happying way with each other. My mom was born in the year of the dragon and my dad was born in the year of the Ox. Dragon lived in heaven and Ox lived on earth. Heaven and earth were two disconected worlds and usually conflicted with each other. They said my mom and my dad had to separated for a long period of time or else one of them, faith would make ceasing. That what I heard from people. It was scary to hear and I didn't believe in what people said faith. However, as I grew up I had witnessed many situations just like my mom and dad. There was a woman, one of my mom's friends. Her age was my mom's age and her husband was my dad's age. They were together happy, but her husband died after she had the first child and three of my neighbors experienced the same situation. My grandma said, "Their life ended up death because they were against faith." I didn't know what to believe any longer.

Living in America, whenever my mom and my dad argued to each other; I usually called my half-sister or my aunts talking about my parents. I thought about my aunts would solve the problems between my mom and dad, but I was wrong. My aunts' families had their own problems too. They didn't want to stick their noses in someone else business. I used to witnessed my mom using one of my dad's ties tightened his neck trying to kill him because she was jealous. Every woman is jealous, but jealous in a wise way is hard because not many can hold their tempers in jealousy situation. My mom's observation about my dad was right, but her actions were not right and wise enough to defense her temper.

My dad was a type of man who would never listen to others especially his family, but to conquer his heart was an easy job that people rarely discovered in a conservative man. I just had to listen and do what he said or being soft to him I could melt his heart. However, I was the one who was not easy to persuade by others unless I wanted to. I, once, had promised to myself never listening to my dad. Now I knew It was time for me to adjust myself to dad. Adjusting to dad, I could remind him the special daughter he had. My dad wanted to see his mistakes by himself rather than others tried to correct him. It was true that trying to see your own mistakes was very hard, but at least you tried. When my dad bragged about himself, he did not harm people. I left my family so many times, but I promised myself I never harmed my family. Most of the times, I was arguing with my dad because of his cold and conservative personality. I finally realized that I had to learn how to forgive people. All the incidents in my life were not his faults, but it was life. My parent never comforted me, but they let me see the progress of life. I never wanted to learn the perfection of life, but learning was different from becoming. I didn't want to learn to become "Perfect".

My Father

There must always be a struggle between a father and son while one aim at power and other at independence.

Samuel Johnson War separated the man who should give paternal care for me. He wiped his tears to leave his daughter finding her a better future. The sea waves screamed miserably blending with his desperation on his escaping way. He cried of missing his wife, his child, and his beloved country. He seized with grief and howled bitterly along with the sea waves until hoarse. Now, he whispered, "My daughter was here with me now, but why life was still not giving me a moment of happiness or peace?" I cried, "No, if you are happy while I was depressing. Life was not fair." I wanted to see him cried like the day he left me, so he knew how I cried bitterly without him. There was something in my heart that I would never forgive him; not until the tamarind leaves stop being sour and bitter.

03

My dad left Vietnam when I was a one-year-old baby. I had no memory about him at all. In Vietnam, nobody ever showed me his picture. They just said that I was a replication of him. I didn't care about his absence that much. He was either with me or not with me, my feeling for him never changed. I always had the feeling of being aborted by my father because he had a betrayal wife. Sometimes, my maternal grandma told me about how flirty my dad was to other girls when he already married to my mom. I hated dad not because of what my maternal grandma had told me but because I didn't know who he really was and looked like. My maternal grandma told me my dad was a player, perhaps, she wanted to prove why my mom remarried and my maternal grandma's defensive words tried to say that my mom wanted to get equal to whatever my dad had done to my mom. I never blamed mom for anything that she had done wrong. I just blamed her why she had to hurt herself living in this unperfect society, everyone was probably full of guilts. For some reasons that I could never figure out why Dad never replied back to any of my letters. He did not care about his daughter's feeling of losing a father because there wasn't attachment in the beginning anyhow. My maternal grandma told me to write for him many times, but I did not know what to say in the letters. I did not know anything about my own dad. All I knew about him was what my grandma said my dad was a player. I did not live with him or know about his looked since I was a baby. The attachment between father and daughter had not existed in me. I wondered if dad ever tried to contact me or respond to any of my letters. Dad's absence gave me a feeling that he did not care for me that much, why would I care about him? If I wrote a letter with my true thoughts to Dad, I didn't have money to send. However, If my maternal grandma sent out my letters, I had to write what she dictated. Sometimes, I did not want to write but grandma forced me. I was sick of writting for dad because all the letters mainly asking for money. I still remembered all the letters repeattedly the word "Money"; "Dad, I felt sad without money. Could you send me some money? I needed money for school. My friends had their parents gave money for their needs." That was an embarrasment because the sadness of missing dad had nothing to do with asking for money? The important thing was money; so it reminded my dad sending money to feed me. My thought was a responsible man did not need to be reminded as being a father. I did not know dad concern about my existence or not, I never got any answered back from him. A lot of times I had a feeling my dad regretted to have me in this world because thinking of me he would think about mom. Mom took another step beyond his expectation. At first, dad probably thought mom would be faithful to him since mom saw me everyday. If I was there with mom and mom still decided to take another step, that assumed I was useless and mom did not care about dad anymore. I was a lonely child who did not know my dad's appearance and his responsibility. I lost trust in my dad.

However, dad was not heartless as I thought. He sponsored mom, my half-sister, half-brother, and me to America. He was a generous man. Sometimes, I asked myself did my dad really forgive my mom or he sponsored my mom here because my paternal grandpa asked him so? Still I could not feel his thought and live with him long enough to understand him thoroughly. I started my life with dad when I was about sixteen years old. Although my appearance looked very much like him, Dad and I had different aspects of life. Socially, dad always looked neat, gentle, happy, and very nice. He was an egotism who always thought and talked about him as a great deal. At home, he always looked grouchy, grumpy, and quiet. He was strict and a conservative man. Dad wanted to control over his family. When the family had been under his control, he expected the family to be what he wanted to be; not the way the member wanted. He always thought his decision was right. I did not mean his mind was limited or he was an old fashion man. I always obeyed my dad because my life seemed forever depending on him, but I was not respected him. In my mind, any day I was still depending on him, I still had to listen to his rules. Dad left me since I was a baby. In his mind, I still was a little child that needed to be trained carefully. His training way was not fitted for a mature girl like me. Everytime my friends called; Dad said I was not home even though I was at home all the times. I was sitting next to him and my friend called me on the phone. My dad picked up the phone and said, "She is not home". I didn't understand how old is it to be elegible to talk on the phone. I went out all the times since he told my friends I was not home; plus I did not want to invite my friends home to see dad's grouchy face. At the first time I lived with dad, I felt like I was backing to the old place again where I used to confront with my maternal grandma. Dad wasn't cruel like my maternal Grandma, but he could make one mentally die by his headstrong. Evevy time I went out with dad and his friends, I always heard his friends bragged about how good their children were as doctors or engineers. Dad did not have anyone to brag and he had to lie to avoid losing face in the community. All those times, I felt so guilty and depressed for not achieving anything to make him proud of me. Sometimes, I cried inside and whisperred to dad, "Do you embarrassed with your friends because I'm not a doctor or an engineer, but it never could be because good heart or soul had to see inside. I rarely went with dad to any of his friends' houses. Maybe Dad loved me more when people bragged about their children because he felt sorry for me. I was not lucky enough to be what I wanted to be like other children. That was the reason why I should be the one who my dad loved and cared more than anyone else.

One time, one of my aunts told me about her childhood without a father. She said, "Whatever my dad did don't against him because having father was still better than not having a father." My dad was her oldest brother and represented the role of a father who should take care of my aunt since my paternal grandpa died of cancer at the age of fifty five. Once, my aunt got home late from a party. My dad wanted a girl to have a curfew because it was very dangerous for a girl to go outside at night. All the rape cases reported to the police each day even day time. My dad used a twig to whip my aunt. She was so angry and ran away from home for three days. My paternal grandma was so worried. My dad told my paternal grandma that my aunt would come back anytime and it was true. My aunt came back home saying sorry to my dad and admitted her fault. My dad said when he yelled or whipped someone that meant he loved and cared for that person. If he did not yell, or whip, or regard to that person at all that meant he gave up and had no way to discipline that person any longer. I wondered if his discipline way was right! He never whipped me, but I still ran away from home. Was it meant he did not care about me any longer? I came back home because I always remembered what my maternal grandpa said, "Wherever I go, no one would treat me better than my family." I gave myself a try returning back to my family, but I was always depress for my dad cold face without any words to me.

To be discipline was to be able to help the children in an order of a family. Dad taught me all the rules of a family and maintained the tradition. He said, "Maintain the tradition and obey the family's rules were the first school for any diligent child" Dad meant according to the Vietnamese tradition; a loyal Vietnamese daughter had to meet four virtuous qualifications: Cong, Dung, Ngon, and Hanh. "Cong" meant my housework had to be completed and organized strictly each day. "Dung" meant my appearance had to be neat and clean; not necessary to be pretty. "Ngon" meant my language had to be thorough and tender; before making any response to a converstion, I had to think carefully. If I weren't munching before I swallowed, I would be considered an airhead. "Hanh" meant good

conduct. I had to discipline myself before I could act to a necessary situation. I had to be able to control the anger to gain respect and wisdom. My
dad usually said, "A wise man does not solve a problem in anger, but in
diplomacy."

I never opposed my dad for teaching me about all the virtuous qualifications of a traditional woman. I agreed with Dad that performance of a
Vietnamese woman I definitely always dreamed to be. Had you ever
depressed for could not achieve any dream that your dearest father wanted
you to be? Like I told every body, I took matter very serious. All the time I
tried to obey Dad's rules, but I was desperately fail. I argued against dad
and ran away from home. My thought was not my dad's thought. Both of
us created a fatal matter that never could be explained. My heart was not
his heart since the day he left me in Vietnam. Dad and I were happy to
learn that we were unhappy when sat down trying to solve all the miserable
pasts. He made me felt like an abandon child when I was in Vietnam. I
abandoned him because I did not have a father-daughter love feeling
between him and me. Dad and I were not in the same path and could never
be. I could never be his diligent daughter because he created an ugly creature. The ugly creature defined her own heart and soul against him. I
always felt hopeless and useless when I was a little girl. Since I was with
dad, he added up more in me; I could not be good as the way he expected
me to be. He wasted all his efforts to teach me right and wrong. Destiny
really not brought us together, but it was because of my mom. He was with
me or not with me, it did not really matter to me. I did care when mom
was not around me because mom reminded me a phrase, "Nobody perpect,
nobody belongs to anybody." I did what I thought It was right for me. I
didn't do what people thought it was right for me. People said my dad was
a generous man. I thought so. If I was my dad, I would never sponsor my
step-children next to me. Dad was great, but he used his greatness maltreat
my mom's heart to climax. He didn't respect my mom that much because
he never listened to my mom ideas even though people said two mind was
better than one. He never listened how could he know my mom was wrong

and without wrong nobody could learn the right things. People in the family was depended on him that was why he thought his decision was important and all the dependants had to follow no matter it was right or wrong. Maybe I underestimated dad because he could be good at the heart without showing his feeling. Dad looked cold and grouchy all the time, but inside I could melt his heart anytime by being sweet to him. As I said, Dad and I were not in the same path and I was sorry to say that there was not any attachment between us since I was a little girl.

Dad told me about the father and son experiences in his life. When dad was young, he asked his parent for money to buy books for school. His parents did not care to ask why he wanted the money. His parent resisted giving him so. Nobody in the family had gut to ask his parent for money. I didn't understand what dad really wanted me to get out from his story, perhaps, from my thought he wanted to warn me did not ask for the money and I had to earn money by myself. I was pleased because dad taught me to be independent. No one in the family included my half-sister and half-brother ever asked my dad for money. He only gave when he was pleased and his attitute was the fear that stopped people who had thoughts asking him for money. No one knew how much he earned or any financial information about him. My dad was extreme quiet about his personal account to his family. I didn't know why I never wonderred. Perhaps, I never knew anything about him anyhow that was my thought. Trying to understand my own dad was hard right now for me because I was a woman right now and I had my personal life too. That was how I always tried to find an old man with my dad's character.

One day, I went to my Dad's office and heard his secretary told me that, "Your dad gave me money for books to school. He said I could take sometimes off for legal classes." Hearing the secretary's sweet voice, I didn't know what to think anymore. The mix feeling about my dad was all over my head. I whispered to myself, "He never gave me money for school. Maybe, I wasn't follow his rules" Dad was a thoughtful, caring, and sweet dad; beside he always wanted the family to follow his way, not the family's way. That people said, "Stubborn". Dad loved me very much. Sometimes I looked back and amazed to see all the caring he did for me when I was ill in bed. Nobody could ever care for me as much as he did. According to the Vietnamese tradition, a gentleman also required to have at least three qualifications that were Humanity, Courage, and Trust. In a family, a husband had to consider himself to have the Humanity to love his family and others. He had to have Courage to protect his family and help others. He also had to keep trust to get credit and confidence from people. In behavior and accommodation with people, "Trust" is a very important factor. From two qualifications, Humanity and Courage, you could see the respectable appearance in a man in a family; also outside the society. When a man had Humanity and Courage, inside his family never happenned the cruel things. Because Humanity is love from the heart; Courage is the power coming from the spirit and energy to control anger into ill-bred person. A man without Courage could not protect a family because running a home is harder than governing a country. Confucius said, "Govern a country is easy like playing an instrument. Running a home is like holding the reins of the horse." Trust, this qualification was not only important in the family, it was also important outside society. Confucius said, "A person doesn't have trust in himself will not know what he must do and what to do"; Also he said, "A man who has trust in himself like a car with strong wheels. A trustful man says one word like a horse with one whipped signal, one whip could never stop the horse from running; a man with one word already said, he could not take it back." A trustful man usually shows his qualification in his faithfulness and loyalty. A man with no Trust sooner or later people will get away. My maternal grandpa often said to me when he still alived, "King and official without trust to each other, the country is not in peace. Father and Children without trust to each other, the family is dysfunctional. Brothers and sisters without trust to each other, love is not completed. Friends without trust to each other, communication is fate away." My dad had Humanity and Courage in himself, but I was afraid he didn't have trust in himself or I believed I didn't trust my own father. I think that why my family became a dysfunctional family. My dad bought that picture in the auction for thousand dollars, but he forgot he had not paid me as I worked as a receptionist for him. I had my bills to pay too, but I would work free for him if he really didn't have any money. I felt pity for myselt when I suspected my own father. I didn't know I should or should not have corrupt thought in me. I thought he intended to buy the picture and not paying me to work for him because he wanted to get risk of me. He had to pay to hire other receptionist anyway. Well, I felt bad when I thought bad about my Dad and distrust him, but I couldn't stand to see the way he spent money for others and not paid me while I worked for him.

My dad business was helping disable people and he had helped thousand of disable people applying for Social Security Disability Benefit. The depressing thing was that he couldn't help his own daughter. Is she too young? Is she educated? I am his daughter and I have seizure for seven years. My condition is not too bad compare to other severe one and I can't drive. I had studied in University and they had to bring me home often either from the classrooms or from the hospital because the seizure had struggled me down. I stayed home, but I had seizure during showers that gave me black eyes and bruces all my body. My mom and dad couldn't stay home watching me. My dad took me to work with him answering the phone calls. One day, I answered a call from one of my dad clients. The client's wife was mentally ill and he did all the paper works for her. The SSA office denied his claim because his wife didn't go to any doctors' examination. The clients came in asking me if I had any way to help him making his mental wife to go to the doctor. The client said every time he took his wife to doctors' examinations, she rebelled violently against him. The appointment had to be cancelled so many times, but the SSA office didn't know her serious sickness. The claim was denied. The client cried in an acrid voice for help; he thought my dad was god or something. What could I say to the client? My dad could not help his own daughter, how could he help you! or the Social Security office, they didn't care how severe you are. You asked them for money and your part was you have to follow their paper work's procedures. Some of the clients died during they were applying for their sickness and after all, their closed relatives received the money for them. It was pity and sorry. I told my dad that I could have died in the shower or at work some day before they consider I qualify for the Social Security Disability Benefit. Similar like one of my dad's client, the mental disorder woman; she almost killed herself, spent months in mental hospital for severe disorientation, and sadness had impaired her normal functioning life. Her doctor even said she seriously needed help too, but she just missed one doctor appointment from the Social Security office; they resisted her saying that she had insufficient doctor's evidents. Her yearly medical doctor reports, they said insufficient; and their one day medical doctor report they determined that sufficient. I didn't know what to think; my seizure is serious and medications could control it. Why didn't they think where the hell I get the dam money to buy medications for my seizure if I could not work? Is it easy for a seizure disorder woman to find a job? I was not mentally ill like the woman. My dad said he didn't let me drive for the reason that if I have seizure during my driving; if accident happen to others, I would feel guilty for all my life and as a father he would have to be responsible. We didn't want that to happen and to avoid the tragic I just didn't drive at all. I just listened to dad and depressingly depended on him for he always said to people if he was not hired me to work for him no one would hire me and his voice was like without him I would be nothing. I envisioned I was back to the old place and heard the cruel voice of my grandma again and again. My dad had too much pride in himself. My dad had too much responsibilities on me that he could not handle and out of his expectation. However, he didn't know the way to make me disappear completely. I guessed he probably entered on all his christmas list that one day I never wake up on my sleep forever. I stayed home because of my mom and my little brother. My dad usually argued with my mom blaming her or his family gave him too much distress while many perfect women waiting for him to have a new happy life with them.

The true reason I guessed he had not responsible for anyone for sixteen years; He knew my mom only for two years when they married to each other and then he left to America. Dad and Mom's relationship was missing something. When they separated, each person managed their own life. After sixteen years reunited, they wouldn't listen to each other. Each person wanted to be their own management and personality didn't match. Argument bursted out that made the dysfunctional family into tears. Dad never knew where my heart really was; he never knew my heart was in this family because I never had one that I always wished in my heart I would die for it.

I felt I was bitter like a tammarind leaf. I was free from my cruel grandma. I was free to see my life as a lunatic, but yet I was distrust my real dad each day. If I did not trust my own parent, whom would I trust? I felt all the people around me were the cruel creatures. Grandpa! Give me strength to be wise and strength to accept myself to continue the adventure of my life. I learned what it meant to forgive, forget, and foreahead.

The Convent

I missed the convent not because it's elegant architecture. It was because the convent like a wonderful spirit reminding me a time that I always specially wanted to save times in a bottle. It was a spritual gift of my life that I ever forgot. Everything was past, but I thought it was just happenned yesterday. Ten years had passed, the tamarind buds had grown over and over again. I was in United States, but one morning I thought I was in the Convent (Vietnam) because I dreamed I saw those tamarind leaves fell all over me like rain. I remembered my third wish when I sat inside the convent that I could wear a white long dress going along those green tamarind leaves. This is 20th century, who could be the fair lady who granded me the third wish, a very simple ordinary wish. Only a dream could grand me that ordinary wish.

04

When I was about thirteen years old, my mom sent me to a convent, where all the Vietnamese and French speaking nuns lived there. I studied special sewing and embroidery. I loved all my sewing works because sewing and embroidery required creativity and a lot of patient. I was always good at embroidery and the nun that I worked for, who was also my teacher, usually complimented all my embroidered arts on cloth. I never had a chance to visit around the whole convent because most of the area was sanctuary. They prohibited outsider excepted the registered students. I had my own study room. It was a very quiet and small room. The room only fitted an armed chair, a wooden table next to a walking door, and the table was placed under the window; throught the window, I could see the double main door of the convent. The front yard filled with tamarind leaves. It was a peaceful ambiance and my study hour only an hour a day and two hours of practice works. Sometimes I was so tired and walked out the front yard of the convent relaxing for a while. I used to close my eyes standing beside one of the Tamarind trees which grew in front of the convent's gate. It was always a beautiful fall season and I loved to watch all those leaves falling down on the road. Sometimes the street was empty of people and transportations. The tamarind leaves were falling all day and covered the street like a gigantic green carpet. It was a briliant picture and unforgettable moment in my mind. The tamarind leaves also fell all over my head, my hands, and my shoulder followed with a chill of fresh wind. I whispered, wherever I went I would come to this peaceful silence and spiritual place. I would never forget the age of being a school-child. I drove to school daily on my bicycle along those tamarind trees. It was beautiful there like a vivid picture in my mind. I wished I could lived a long speechless life like those tamarind trees in peace. I did not know how old those tamarind trees were, but I was sure they had stood there before my parent even born in this world. My childhood memories came back whenever I thought of those tamarind trees. It liked a film rewinding back in my mind.

Within a tropical weather, Vietnam had only two seasons that were summer and fall. Sometimes, it rained mostly every day during the fall season. I remembered during the daytime my cousins and I used to wear short pants running out the street and playing under the rain. We always so excited and loved the freshness of the water so much during the raining season. One of my bestfriends said raining was a sign to tell people that god was crying because of sadness caused by human. At the teenager age, I did not wonder why my bestfriend had that idea in his mind. I never cared about the silly feeling about the rain that my bestfriend had in his mind. He was five years older than me and was a very handsome young man. I was always happy in the rain with my cousins. We did not care of those people who yelled at us for running around their shops. Rain cleaned us and washed away our day.

I stopped running out the street on the rainy day when I was old enough to understand about my bestfriend's depressing thought in the rain. I realized all the times my lovely bestfriend and I revealed secrets to each other, I felt better. I did not know what love was, but I knew that I had a crush on him. He comforted and protected me when I was lonely. He loved poems and neither I did. I did not know that was true love or not, but he and I always spent times with each other. Unfortunately, I stopped loving him when I found out that he was one of my cousins. His dad was my dad's brother and he was the lost son for twenty years. I wrote diary at the age of fourteen on most of the raining day. I usually looked through the window and whispered that I knew why god was crying all the raining reason. It was because human never stopped making mistakes. I had a big mistake for loving my cousin. According to the Vietnamese tradition, I could not marry to my closed blood cousin. That was restricted for all Vietnamese people and I had to accept attentively. My cousin's father was my dad's younger blood brother. They lost each other during the war and now they found each other after my cousin came to my house. Rain always brought most of my memories together especially this love between my cousin and I. Nevertheless, as my maternal grandpa said, "It was never the end of the world." Every part of the ground where I grew up filled with all my memories. The convent was still there with all my memories together.

My Mother

She thought I talked bad about her life and she felt ashame for herself. However, I learned to be strong and brave through her life's experiences. She made me proud of who I am because I did not make mistakes like her. Is this novel fiction? My mom's life had highlighted a part of this fiction. I would do anything to get her out from the distress. She thought she had lost her heart, but she didn't know that her heart was mine. That was why I never would leave her in any situation of my life.

05

The role of a Vietnamese girl expects to fulfil as she grows up to be a woman is a very difficult task of all. She must contiuously try to establish a good name for her family's ancestor. From the moment, her mind is mature enough to understand commend; she is expected to be a diligent daughter. From the day she is married off; she is expected to be a submissive wife. Morever, from the time she bears children she is expected to be an altruistic mother. My mom's life seemed expecting more from her. What went wrong with her? I thought about that question all the times and I think she did have the same thought as me too. I never believed in faith because I noticed that whenever my grandma was feeling down or worse things happened to her life, she began to blame on faith. Grandma blamed on faith for faith had arranged my mom into a way that mom never expected and that unexpected way forced my mom to accepted the tragic anyway. When I thought about my mom's life, part of her life was what she chose for herself and the other part was created by her fragile personality. My mom never said anything about faith. Human had weakness, but how human handled the restriction in themselves. That was the important matter of all. Was it true that faith had arranged my mom to be that way? I suspected. Her parent never expected or forced her into anything. What they wanted my mom were to take care of her and to have a relaxed life. She was old enough to care for herself and her parent asked her to be strong so she could be able to think for herself sometimes. Was she had the ability to make her life as the way her parent asked? Mom thought her life was simple, but looking through the way that her life had been through I only saw few in this life. Sometimes I asked myself, how she had all that decisions in her mind? Did she pick up her sadness from faith? I didn't ask her directly because I knew she was a sensitive woman. Anything that related to her personal life, she could stir up angry anytime and do unexpected actions without any control.

My mom thought so much about others that she forgot about herself. Forgetting herself, perhaps, could help her off sadness, but mom was wrong that she had been destroying herself each day; she tried continuously working to forget her sadness. She worked from early seven in the morning to ten at night and seven days a week. Instead of becoming a strong woman, mom remained weak as the way she was born to become. Her parent always talked about her fragileness, and sensitiveness. As she got older, she turned into another woman just like my maternal grandma. I guessed because she experienced the same sadness as maternal grandma after her husband left. However, mom didn't cruel like grandma, but my maternal grandma didn't act crazy like my mom on the way. Each person received their own character but same personal life experience. Mom could whine all day and get angry at anytime, but she never hit me when she got mad. I got headache of my mom yelling sometimes, but I understood that her yelling could release the sadness of my dad's absence. I guessed. My dad left my mom an one-year-old daughter in lonliness.

My mom is a skinny woman and about five feet four inches. She has a perfect light brown skin. People said whoever got tanning skin is healthy. I don't think so. Mom was only one hundred pounds and never gain or loose any after bearing her four children. She had serious allergy that bordered her all the times when she lived in Vietnam. People always thought she was crying all the times because she had permanent running nose with a sorrowful face. That was why sometimes I did not know she was crying for her life or because of her allergy. When mom whined aloud, I could see her veins stretching out of her neck. I was afraid that someday those veins could snap into tiny pieces. When mom got angry she always lost control of yelling and doing all fool actions.

Mom is the oldest in the family and the prettiest among all my aunts. She has a unique and modest beauty. When I see my mom picture since she was married my dad, I thought there was another Audrey Hepburn (the actress). My mom and the actress, Audrey Hepburn are like the twin. Being a rich and beautiful woman, she was never being arrogance with anyone. She loved to help people and expected nothing from them. Being young, pretty, and lovely, however, did not bring her life any better but made her life more miserable. Vietnamese people often said the more lovers you had, the much lonely you are. All the men who loved her had their own characteristics and charms. One of her lottery picked numbers was my dad.

My mom and my dad separated during the Vietnamese war in 1975 when I was only an one-year-old baby. Life became very difficult for my mom when my dad left Vietnam. Mom was deep in sorrow each day and never had any thought she could unite with my dad again someday. Dad went to America to escape from the Communist and mom was left back in Vietnam. That was an ocean away from each other. My dad left when mom was a twenty-three years old beautiful woman with full of life. Being in a long distance relationship and having the thought of impossible way to reunite with my dad. It was so hard for my mom to resist the tempta-tion of another love. I could feel her love for my dad slipped away each day. The feeling of losing her husband made mom becoming a love fool. Because of seeing my dad was an illusion of hope, mom decided to settle down with another man. Mom could not determine her own destination. I felt mom's pain from her actions. It was downhearted for me to imagine the depressed feeling from mom when she was being lonely in pain and carried a one-year-old daughter. After all, mom could not fight against her weakness and chose another step for her, remarried. Some people could fight against their medications, but my mom had to take painkiller. Mom's face always showed sadness. There are medications that can cure sickness, but there are no medications can cure the person who fell in a stage of lovesick. My mom remarried to a doctor after my dad. She, perhaps, thought I needed a father and she needed a soulmate. My mom illegally married to a doctor and carried another baby girl when I was three years old. My maternal grandpa was so angry with my mom and dismissed her out off the house. Mom moved out with her new husband. I lived with mom after she remarried, but it was not for long. For some reasons, I didn't know mom and the doctor separated after a year my half-sister was born. I felt sorry for mom, I but couldn't do anything to help. However, mom still had a little hope to get back again with the doctor because my mom got another boy with him when my half-sister was two years old. My half-brother could be the one who carried the doctor's gene. I was wrong about my thought all the way. Men in the 20th century don't care about the responsibilities. The doctor hid away from mom and didn't care about his children any longer. Mom returned to her parent's home when my maternal grandpa escaped to America. My maternal grandma accepted my mom to stay into her house. My maternal grandma helped mom to babysit my half-sister, half-brother, and me so my mom could go to work. Mom started to work like wild. She did not care about her health or her kids. She sewed and knitted all day without feeling exhausted. Sometimes, she stopped working for a while because blood came out from her mouth while she coughed. However, she still kept on working anyway. She did not care about her life anymore. Once, I remembered sitting near my mom's bed and saw her lying there with her weak, pale face, and skinny body. I was so scared and sobbed when I also saw mom coughing with blood came from her mouth constantly and no doctor there for her.

There was another doctor near by my house. He was also one of my mom friends, but my maternal grandma forbid me to ask that doctor for help. My maternal grandma suspected that mom had affair with that doctor also. I did not know that was true or not, I just wanted to save my mom's life. I ran out to meet that doctor. Unfortunately, my maternal grandma caught me at the stair on the way I ran out asking for help. She slapped me and said I poisoned my mom. So many days, I had nightmares that mom could be gone anytime. I started to hate my dad so much. I felt helpless and useless. I blamed my dad for giving a helpless daughter like me in this world. I hated the doctor who was my half-sister's father; he was not deserved to be a doctor. I thought the obligation of a doctor was to help and to be there with the patients. My mom was one of his patients and he wasn't be there with her. How could other patients rely on him when he didn't even care for his own wife. The doctor knew my mom was sick. Even though he did not love my mom anymore, he still had to hold the responsibility of a father. If husband and wife didn't love each other, they still had to have responsibility and value in themselves. Stopping by visit my mom was not a hard job, but the doctor did not have a responsibility and value in him at all. He was not deserved to be a father. I never thought about a father did not want to see his own children. He was garbage and a trash that no one would pick up for recycling. I wished I could spit on his face and said that an uneducated homeless had more human touch and ethical behavior than a doctor did. The most important matter in any human being was that they had to learn the ethical behavior and humanity task in themselves first; then beginning to achieve the education. An educated human who did not have humanity and ethical behavior was an animal, but an uneducated human had humanity and ethical behavior is a complete human. What made my mom became so ill? She didn't do any harm to any of her husbands. If they didn't love her anymore, at least they had to have the responsibilities of the fathers. She couldn't take care of the kids all by herself. To feed and educate the children were not an easy job. Mom wasn't strong enough to handle a family in a smooth way. For all reasons, mom's grief hid in her each day and nothing could chase her shadow away. Mom's personality changed each day. Sometimes, she was yelling all day and did not know what she was really doing. Anyone that made her mad, she would lose control of her anger. She swore all the worse language that only for low-class laborers or streetwalkers. Her voice sometimes was very sweet like sugar, sometimes it was sour like lemon, and several of times it was bitter like her desperate life. Fifteen years striking through desperation and feeding her three children, mom's heart was a permanent scar. Her heart and her mind were not stronger through her experiences but they got weaker each day. Like a potato got smashing down, mom got smashing down by her desperating life. She got drown in the ocean and became a mentally ill woman. Why did I say the worse words like that to my mom? Perhaps, I was the one observed and understood her life enough to discuss about her.

Mom united with my dad after fifteen years living in Vietnam. I guessed she came to America because she thought about the future of her children. They had full of life ahead. America had the best education in the world. I did not know what to think. If I were mom, I would embarrass when I saw my dad. When I made decision to settle down with another man, I didn't have the heart to love my former husband anymore. Mom's two kids were the faults that everyone had obviously seen. I was not agreed when mom lived together with dad after fifteen years separated. They were together anyhow. Maybe the feeling was different and my mom & dad knew the bond between them. Nothing was perfect. It was hard to make a vase, but it was easy to break it. You spent one hour to make a vase, but you could break the vase only in seconds. In relationship, it also likes the making of the vase. Mom and dad had build up their life together, but their life had broken like a vase. After all, they were trying to connect each pieces of their broken life together. People made mistakes each day and their life still went on as long as they knew how to fix their mistakes.

Mom had a scar and it could never be erased. Seeing her scar each day made her mind losing in the crowd. She started to do all the actions that she did not realize that could harm her, not her enemy. Her jealousy killed her. She was jealous with my dad's co-worker. My dad's co-worker was a pretty woman and her name is Lilian. Lilian always wanted to be a model, but somehow she fell that she was not qualifying enough. She obsessed with herself by hanging all her pictures in her office. She dressed completely sexually stimulated. She had a big size breast. When she bent down to reach her things, you could see her whole size breast. She always dressed very sexual stimuli. However, I didn't think she was trying to seduce my dad, especially an old man like my dad with less money. Lilian had many handsome, young, and rich men falling for her. She was usually in my dad office to discuss about problems in working. I knew a man and a woman in an office alone would give anyone a wrong thought in mind. I understood dad's personality and knew what they discussed about. Mom did not understand that the way Lilian dressed could only show her as a low-class pitch. Why would mom jealous with a low-class pitch when she could prove herself as a submissive wife and a caring mother? If Lilian could really seduce my husband, then the man that called my hushand was not my hushand. If I decided to marry a man, that man had freedom to play with any girls as long as he still responsibled for his family. Perfection was makeup of broken perfection.

Mom swore and insulted Lilian in front of the people in the public. She wanted to prove that she was right about Lilian's seduction to my dad. Who saw Lilian seduced my dad? People only saw my mom's anger and whispered that mom insulted herself for having and ignoble husband. Her behavior was over react that proved herself as an uneducated and ignorant woman. Lilian was nothing compared to mom. Mom's beauty was what Lilian wished to have. One thing Lilian was wiser than mom that she knew how to calm an angry man. My dad would melt for any sweet words that could calm him down. Lilian's voice was what people called sweet like "Sugarcane" and my mom's voice was what people called sour like "Lemon". If mom knew she was wrong, she would not do jealousy actions. If Lilian knew she was wrong, she would not dress like a pitch. Mom and Lilian were the broken perfection that made my dad became a perfect man. Through mom and Lilian encounter, people whispered that my dad must be a modest man in order for two beautiful and wise women pulled about.

Curiosity

Curiousity killed the cat.
Satisfaction brought it back.
Saying

Wonder is a state of mind in which…nothing is taken for granded…Each thing is a surprise; being is unbelievabe. We are amazed not only at particular values and things but also at the unexpectedness of being as such, at the fact that there is being at all.
Abraham Ioshua Hesshel.

06

In Vietnam at the neighborhood where I lived there was a special kinder-garten teacher. She was one of my neighbors and she loved kids so much. All the children, included me, in the neighborhood envied her tatent so much. She always told us stories about life and most of her telling stories were about ghost. We were scared but somehow we always loved to hear. When she started the story, we held our breath and put all our attention to her eyes. We sat closely and held each other hands tightly. When the story came to the scariest part, we were sweat all over and yelled out loud like hell. Sometimes, I bit my tongue without noticing it and became mute. The kindergarten teacher studied Child Development and she perhaps observed children's psychology through us. We always wanted to hear her ghost stories with our curiosity. All the times, I wondered why she always had plenty of stories to tell us and never seemed running out of stories. She told us three stories each moonlight day, the night that we always gathered together when the electricity was out. In Vietnam, the electricity was only turned on four days a week. Even though people offered to pay more money, the electric company still did not have enough electric to serve people. I could not count all those ghost stories in all those years that my friends and I were listened to the kindergarten teacher. If she created all those stories, I truly admitted that she was an excellent, and tallented storyteller and also had very good imagination. I would be very proud of that unique in myself if I was her. What was more? Beside listening to those ghost stories, Hide&Seek was usually the game my friends and I used to play. One day, one of my friends was lost somewhere. We tried to find her everywhere almost all night, but we were hopeless. None of us found where she hid. We were frightened to dead and ran home in fear. The fear that ghost could be anywhere beside one of us. One of my uncles told me that ghost could take us away anytime in a Hide&Seek game. I never seemed scare of what my uncle saying. I had never seen a ghost, why should I scare about it? however, if ghost really existed, why would it want to hurt me when I did not doing anything to harm it. Nevertheless, in the morning we saw the girl that we tried to seek all night. She sat under the big tree in front of her house and her mouth was full of clay. All the neighbors said the tree was haunted and the owner was chopped down that tree on the next day. I still didn't understand and surprise why it happenned to that girl. No one could solve that mystery. I just felt secure for her family that at least she was safely back to her home. However, she didn't say any word to explain what had really happen to her. Her personality had changed from that day on. We called her "Mysterious girl". She became violent and evil each day. One of my aunts was one year older than me usually coming over that mysterious girl's house to play with her. That mysterious girl always blamed on my aunt for stealing her stuffs and hit my aunt nonstop. My aunt was a very weak and harmless girl. She could not fight back because that girl was much stronger than my aunt. All my aunt did was running home calling me to help her. I didn't believe until I saw my aunt's bruises on her eyes and her body. I warned that mysterious girl so many times not to hurt my aunt, but she did not pay attention to any of my words. One day, I stopped her in front of her house's back door. I punched her everywhere as she did to my aunt. The mysterious girl ran inside her house to her parent broke down and wept bitterly. Her mom wrapped my arm pulling me to my house and argued with my maternal grandma. She told my maternal grandma taught me how to behave. My maternal grandma did not care to ask what happened; she gave me a big slap on my face. It was so hurt, but I remained silent and glanced at the mysterious girl's hideous eyes; she glanced at me in victory. My aunt didn't say any words but looking at me with her shit eyes. I wished my mom was here with me, but it was just a wish; I had to learn how to defense myself and to deal with the situation later. Parent-child communication was a very important element. To understand my child, I had to observe it every progress of her life. I had no parent to observe my actions or to understand my thought. I knew how an abandoned child felt through the violent mysterious girl encounter. I started to believe that ghost could change people to anything anytime. I kept thinking about ghost had pierced into my maternal grandma, when my maternal grandpa left.

Nevertheless, my maternal grandparent's house was also a scary house. I never had doubt that there was ghost in the house until one day. I was frightenned to death at that time. It occurred in the three story house where I used to live. There was a stair in front of my bedroom's door. The stair connected to the third floor of the house where my uncle used to live. Through my bedroom's window, I saw a man looked like my oldest uncle wearing a short pant without shirt. I was curious my uncle always stopped by my room for a hello before going to his room upstair. This time, he tried to run so fast upstair that I could imagine he was catching a thief running away. I ran out my room. From down stair, I saw a man hid lighting a cigarette behind the wall that divided the balcony door and the room. He tried to played with fired and I began to worry. when I ran upstair, I had no longer seen the man behind the wall. I tried to recover myself back from the situation whether I was dreaming or not, but I could not be dreaming. I headed straight to my uncle's room and he was there sleeping like a dead person. If that man was not my uncle, who was the man behind the wall? Where did he go? If it was my uncle, how could he run back to his room so fast and by which way? I was standing at the stair at all the times and there was no second way to go to my uncle's room. I was stunned and mute like cat got my tongue. This time, it was where I lived and I could not explain the situation.

Furthermore, there was a cemetery near my house that my friends and I usually went there to sit playing on those tombstones. We often played with one kind of topical seeds which we only found to grow in the cemetery. We usually deepened the seeds into our spits and those seeds automatically popped up like the tiny firecrackers. It was very fun to play with those seeds and I could only find those seeds depending on the season, which was summer. One day of the summer, I went to the cemetery and intended to find my friends there. I didn't know what I had in mind at that time, but I never went to the cemetary alone without any of my friend. I crossed the funeral home right in the front of its main door. I saw a dead kid lying on a piece of wood. The dead body had stiffened; the stinky smell combining with the yellow fluid came out from the corpse. It was so nasty that I walked away after a minute observing to fulfill my curiousity. However, when I was far from the funeral house about 1/4 mile, I heard a very loud noise like someone dropping a bomb in there. I ran back to the funeral home, but the corpse was no longer on the piece of wood. It just disappeared. Nobody was there although I kept calling inside the funeral home. It was an empty place and I could not understand what was going on there. I still kept searching for an answer to my questions. Where was the body gone? What was the loud noise? Why there wasn't anybody in the funeral home? I measured from my standing place to the funeral home was about 1 minute running. If people took away the corpse, they could not run that fast away, could they? I wondered each day about what I had witnessed by my own eyes. I asked myself, "Would people going to believe me when I told them what happened?" They probably laughed at me and said I was silly girl. Well, although I didn't have parent beside to take care me properly, I still had the memorable childhood memory that nothing in my life could be better.

My Grandpa

Grandpa! I was a girl, who never wished to be born in this world, but some-how life had reserved for me a space and I survived. Life did not let me give up like you never wanted your family giving up. Life made me striking through all the aspects that I had no choice to resist. Yet a girl like me never believed in faith now facing faith without knowing it until one day; she amazed that she had grown. Grandpa! You lived forever in my heart and I would learn to strike through my life as the way I treasured you.

07

My maternal grandpa left when I was about six years old, but all the memories of him never faded away in my mind. Sometimes, I sobbed to myself because I never had a chance to say how much he meant to me. He left so early and I was so little to understand about him or to reveal my feeling for him. He worked so hard to take care his family and he deserved the words, the best grandpa in the world. He ruled the family with an iron hand. My maternal grandpa was a very successful accountant. He worked for the 3M company and traveled around the world before 1975. All the family's members depended on him for living survival. Since he had gone, the family was deep in trouble of financial problem.

My maternal grandpa had a very hot temper, but most of the time he controlled his temper very well. When he got angry, he must had a very critical reason for his punishment. Most of the time as far as I remembered, he was angry because my grandma spoiled my uncles. In my mom's family side, I had only two uncles. Grandma had an old fashion thought that two of my uncles were the only two who could maintain the family generation. Grandma usually prepared dinners or lunches and brought to my uncles's bedrooms. My maternal grandpa said that was not the right way because grandma was not a servant. If my uncles loved their mother, they should understand and would not let grandma served them like that. If my uncles wanted to eat, they just came down eating with other family members. Nobody would stop them to go down eating. If eating was a hard job for both of my uncles, what would they do in the future without grandma? That action was not a man's movement. In fact, only a loser did that kind of response. My uncles were lazy to come down eating and grandma was scare for they would starve to death. My maternal grandpa said, "Let them starve and then they will come down and eat. If starving does not move them; let them die. I do not have that kind of sons in my family. What kind of men who could not even responsible for their eating?" My maternal grandpa was right. My uncles came down eating after all, but my oldest uncle whispered some bad words that maternal grandpa suddenly heard. My maternal grandpa had never angry at the mealtime unless there must be a very serious matter. I admired maternal grandpa very much in solving problems because all his words were usually very reasonable and fair. All my family members were also agreed about that. At that time, he was so angry to my uncle that he stood up reaching to a thick and long twig near by the dinner table. I was sitting next to my maternal grandpa and his bow of rice poured all over me when he punched hard on the table. I did not cry, but my eyes wide opened in frighten. My uncle tried to run away from the dinner table because he knew he was impolite. My maternal grandpa chased after my uncle, but my maternal grandma blocked in front of grandpa. MY maternal grandma cried and whined begging maternal grandpa not to whip my uncle. The begging helped my uncle from being whip but it made my maternal grandpa's anger going to extreme. My maternal grandpa pardoned my uncle, but whipped my maternal grandma for spoiling my uncle unconditionally not in the right time. My maternal grandpa said, "All my life, I never hit any woman and this is the first time I witness a woman who resists her own race to defense a male character and gets whipping by her own man. All of you watch and learn."

My maternal grandpa loved all his family, but loving meant discipline. He was strict, but that did not mean he did not have a heart to feel pain. Maternal grandpa usually said, "To be a successful leader, a man must cultivates virtue and moral in himself first, then strongly manages his household. When two of those above work successfully, he can govern fairly a country. If the citizens respect and obey him, the leader, peace will come to the country."

Dismissed my mom out of the house was a very hard decision for my maternal grandpa. However, if he neglected the rule in the family, others would repeat the same mistake and would not take his words seriously. Maternal grandpa discharged my mom out of the house for three main reasons. First, she was pregnant to another man illegally after my dad left. War and chaos separated my mom and dad, not my dad wanted to leave my mom. Second, my mom was not faithful to her husband not for long. Third, she brought embarrassment to the family. Since my mom got discharged from the house, grandpa was very frustrated. He did not talk that much and usually sit alone all night outside the balcony. He forbid anyone in the family seeing my mom, but deep inside I knew my maternal grandpa pretended not to know anything about my aunts secretly coming to help my mom. A strictly discipline was not a hatred, but it was a learning lesson or an experience. My maternal grandpa's heart was unique and the one who undertood him could feel the loving from him. After my mom painful experience, maternal grandpa used to tell me that I never knew what tragic would come to life. The best way to avoid the tragic was always prepare for the tragic.

My maternal grandpa hated the Communist. He planed with my uncle-in-law attempted to cross the border of Vietnam to the concentration camp in Thailand. Over there, the U.S. Embassy would protect and help the refugees with all their generosity. Since the day Grandpa and my uncle-in-law had escaped from Vietnam, I never heard from grandpa again. No one found his body or heard anything about him. My uncle-in-law, the one who escaped with grandpa, told me about their trip. They walked to the border between Campchia and Vietnam. At the border, thousand of the bullets flied upper their heads. Grandpa told my uncle-in-law crawling across the border first and grandpa would follow after. My uncle-in-law crawed to the other side, which was Campuchia , and waited there for grandpa. However, three days had passed and my uncle-in-law didn't hear any sign from grandpa. My uncle-in-law was starving to death, but thinking about his wife he continued his trip otherwise he could have died for waiting. From that day, everybody assumed that grandpa had gone forever, but he never died in my heart.

I was usually by his side everyday and called him daddy. I heard one of my aunts, who was older than me one years old, called grandpa "Daddy" and I just followed her call. I really did not understand what it meant. There was no man beside me accepted grandpa at that time. Nobody explained for me the different between the word "Daddy" and "Grandpa". My aunt said, "He isn't your daddy you fool" I argued to my aunt, "You are older than me just one year old. You can call that mean I can call too. Nothing you can do to stop me." Sometimes, I slapped my youngest aunt on the face for stopping me to call my grandpa "daddy". Now whenever I talked to my youngest aunt about that I felt so silly and rude. Luckily I wasn't lived near my aunt or else I would feel guilty for my violent action on her. I was so innocent and didn't know the different between man and man.

However, grandma tried to correct me not to call grandpa "Daddy", but grandpa did not let her. Grandpa defended me, "Right now, she needs a love of a father. It does not matter who she calls daddy. She will change when she grows up enough to understand." Grandpa told me many fairy tales. As a six years old girl, I never figured out that each fairy tale grandpa told I could learn a precious lesson. I remembered the story of a little mermaid, the stars on the sky, and the boy eating figs under a fig tree.

I was crying when I heard the little mermaid's story, but I alwayd wanted to be a little mermaid though. I envied the little mermaid greatest love of all. She was a woman I always wanted to be because she never regretted what she had done in love. Grandpa and I usually sat together watching the moon and the stars on the sky. He said, "Look at all those stars, when you see a star falls that means a person on earth passes away" Even though grandpa had gone forever, his star never fell, and he never died in me. His star was always shine on the sky. He always lived in my heart and I cherished his words until the day I died.

Another story grandpa told me was about the boy under the fig tree. I could not assume totally grandpa thought because each individual had different point of view. The story was about the boy choosing the best figs to eat under a fig tree. When the boy was full, there was still a big and delicious fig left. The boy still threw the fig away like nothing for him anymore. After the story, I was laughing and said grandpa crazy. Nothing in the story drew my attention. I wondered why grandpa told me a vague story like that. Now, I was in love with a man and I tried to not full of love. I never threw away any love that he gave to me, but I tried not to be fulled of his love. If I was fulled, I would not know what was the best of love like the boy under the fig tree anymore. That was how I related my love to the story. I always wish for something that you don't have, but when I got it; it's not special to me anymore and become vague. Grandpa never told meaningless story. His words always had something behind it. That was all I remembered about my dearest maternal grandpa. He lived forever in my heart as I always cherished my meaningful childhood stories with him.

My Grandma

If we continually try to force a child to do what he is afraid to do, he will become more timid, and will use his brains and energy, not to explore the unknown, but to find the ways to avoid the pressures we put on him. If, however, we are careful not to push a child beyond the limits of his courge, he is almost sure to get braver.

John Holt

08

I hated myself for hating my maternal grandma. She was the one who fed me when my parent was not with me. I wished I did not have the cruel kind of grandma who seemed put all of her hatred on me for no reason. However, without her I would not be survived to grow strong as a mature girl. Maybe I din't hate her anymore, but her cruelty never could erase from my memory. I could never grow up without learning it. My maternal grandma also created a lively fiction in me.

Since the day my maternal grandpa left, grandma cried all day of missing him. She changed to a different woman. She always screamed and whined cruelly each day. At that time, my mom was busy working for living survival. I missed mom everyday because she rarely saw me during the daytime. When my mom got home from work, I was probably sleeping. I hated maternal grandma so much that I thought I could have killed her anytime if I had any chance. I did not know why her behavior was so insane after her husband left. I often waited for mom to go home to protect me from maternal grandma's anger, but mom was so busy with her works. I understood that maternal grandma was deepped in sorrow because the absence of her husband, but I was not a scapegoat of her distress. Every mistake that I made, maternal grandma usually slapped me so hard on my face and whipped me all over my body with a long twig. Sometimes, my body was swelling all over and the slapping of her fingers printed on both of my cheeks. I often sobbed silently and squeezed my hands tightly sitting in the corner of the kitchen. Maternal grandma thought my body made of iron; she thought I could not feel the pain. Grandma was about fifty years old at that time and I was almost thirteen. Maternal grandma's face always filled with makeup that made her face white like a Japanese's Geisha. I never took a chance to observe any detail of her face, but generally, grandma looked very pleasant to people's eyes. I guessed she must be a very pretty woman when she was young. As grandma got older, grandma got fatter. She had a big belly and small feet that made very hard for her to walk. Whether she was pretty or not, she always looked the same to me, a barbarian woman. Most of the time, I helped grandma cooking, washing dishes, and cleaning the house. I did not mind to help. I would appreciate grandma for giving me a chance doing those houseworks because doing houseworks would help me to be an independent woman in the future. I felt I was luckier than many children who begged on the street with no shelter and no work to do. However, those poor children had freedom of their own. I had freedom of bounding myself on the ground begging and hoping grandma granded her generosity heart to me. My freedom was to let her insulting me for I was depending on her charity. Where were my mom and dad? As long as I loved mom, I had to adjust myself to grandma. My mom could not be with me because she had to work so hard to feed me. My life attached me to grandma and I could never deny that truth.

What had I done to deserve all those punishments that maternal grandma granded me? I had no one to share the feeling of being under hatred of grandma. A lot of time I was wailing without any comfort of someone. The story of Cinderella was not a fairy tale for me anymore. I did not have a beauty like Cinderella and never hoped for a prince to rescue me. I believed grandma could possibly abuse me any time as long as I still depended on her. My grandma was like a stepmother and I could not do anything about the abusing actions. I only had a heart to tolerate the pain, a soul to perceive right or wrong and a mind to record the word "Prevention" in my mind. How could I find a prince to rescue me in this

20th century? Did anyone really care about my existance in this world? Every single action grandma did to me; I kept in mind clearly each day. Many times, I just blew out crying and yelled back at grandma without fear, but that did not bring me any good. In fact, my responded words harm me even more than before. It showed no help but made grandma angry at me more. Grandma thought that I offended her. She whipped me as hard as she could and warned me ever reacting that way to her again. I whispered to myself that I could not endure her brutally behavior one day I would kill her. I realized the cruel woman was my grandma and she needed help more than I did. Who would help me? The more I loved grandpa, the more I told myself to endure grandma's cruel actions. Grandpa used to say that it never the end of the world.

My maternal grandma said I was an abandoned child living under her charity. To be an abandoned child was to know my duty of listening and obeying her rules. Grandma whined all day and swore all those dirty words. She called my mom is pitch, my dad is hell and I am barrier. I always wondered if grandma understood what she was really talking about to a teenager girl like me. God was a generous man in this whole world, but I surely believed that even god could not tolerate her dirty language. The language my aunts and I always called "Non-registered foreign" for uncivilized people. Grandma was an adult and she had to be a role model for her grandchildren. I was always frightened whenever I stood up close to grandma. Any mistakes that I made I would receive a slap without any explaination. Her cruel behavior made me collapsing in fear each day. Each day, I used to grandma's brutal behavior. Unfortunately, grandma always had new manner to defeat a pity girl like me.

There was a time; I used to stay up late at night finishing my homework for school beside a table lamp near my bed. Without a word, grandma came inside my room and turned off the light. I said I had to finish the homework for tommorow school, but she gave me a slap on my face and left without any word. I was wailing in the middle of the night and hoped mom would be there with me. I cried because grandma was not fair. One of my aunts could stay up all night to study under the lamp, but I could not. Suddenly, I stopped sobbing because I thought about may be grandma couldn't afford to pay for the electricity or my aunt's homework was more important than mine for she was in college? I had to be optimistic and aware of the situation.

My maternal grandma once asked me what I wanted to be in the future. I answered that I wanted to be a flight attendant. My maternal grandma just laughed out loud and looked at me with a piteous face. She said in order to be a flight attendant I had to be pretty and tallented. I was stunned by her words. Grandma described my face like a monster. I was so terrify to accept the monster she just described was mine. She said my eyed were long like a snake, my mouth was big like a megaphone and my nose was big and long like a chimney. She was not even giving me an encouragement or at least told me that I was not fit in the flight attendant requirements or it was not an easy job like I thought it was. Beside, she made me felt ugly and lost confidence in myself. Her extreme voice filled with hatred. I accepted the truth of being ugly, but an understandable grandma never tried to hurt her granddaughter. I did not understand why she hated me so much and always looked down on me. After that conversation with grandma, I never hoped or dreamed about any of my future goal. whenever I thought of a dream, the fire voice of grandma burned my dream away.

It was never enough for me to tell about grandma's evil actions. Grandma was also a greedy woman. My half-sister used to have a dog bite on her left leg when she crossed one of our neighbor front-yard. The bite was serious but it healed after several weeks without any stitches even though my sister did show some bitterly pain. The owner of that dog felt guilty and usually offered my sister foods and money after the accident. I always resisted those gifts because it was not the owner's fault. One day, she gave me a pack of tiny rice cakes. I could not record back the thought of why I accepted the gift. I took home for my half-sister, but grandma stopped me at the stair asking why I would dare to accept the gift without adult's permission. I backed up one step without any word. I started crying and frightening. I, perhaps, loved to eat those tiny cakes and could not control myself to not accept them. I could not explain my action to grandma because I knew what grandma would do after her lecture. I stood there receiving some slaps from grandma. My truly thought was my half-sister should deserve something for her wound or at least something showed concern from the owner of the dog. They should felt responsible for that accident. I was trembling at grandma and could not explain my thought. Grandma took those tiny rice cakes and ate all by herself. She did not even give my half-sister one bite. I was so mad because my mom paid for the cost of my half-sister dog bites serious injury. My mom did not say anything to the owner at all in stead she advised my half-sister to be careful next time and the wound was an accident. My mom was right, but what about my half-sister scar? She was not deserved the accident and her small benefit went into my grandma's mouth. Was that fair for my half-sister?

My half-sister, who was born three years after me, never could visualized her father's appearance neither I did. I really could not comprehend that fact. After the separation of the doctor and my mom, I had never seen him again. My half-sister's paternal grandpa used to visit my half-sister and my half-brother, who was born six years after me. They were very happy whenever they saw their paternal grandpa. Their paternal grandpa usually took them home for two weeks and returned them back. He was an old man with white hair and gentle as a lamb. When he returned my half-sister and my half-brother, they often had new clothes and happy than ever. Once, their paternal grandpa gave me an amount of money to buy gifts for my half-sister and my half-brother. I did not count that money, but I knew it was quite a lot. I was too little to handle that amount of money and my mom was not home often. I decided to give to my maternal grandma all the money. Grandma said if next time my half-sister's paternal grandpa gave anymore money. I just had to throw back right on his face. I thought she taught me how to obey the elder like I always obeyed her, but she was rude herself. Even though the old man like my half-sister's paternal grandpa made mistakes, I should not throw the money on his face. He did not do anything wrong to hurt me. Grandma was probably angry with my half-sister's father for abandoned his children, but that was not the kids's faults or their paternal grandpa's fault. Grandma often had a way put anger on other people's shoulders. Why grandma was angry at me? Because I accepted money for her own shake. In addition for all those times that grandma fed my half-sister and my half-brother without any financial support! May be she wanted to tell that she did not need their charity, but she had to deal with the situation by her own rather than telling a kid to throw back the money. I considered throwing money on the face of an adult was not a polite action for any kid to experience. After all, grandma took the money and spent for her good instead of spending for my half-sister and half-brother after the long lecture of how to behave. My maternal grandma got to spend the money, but my half-sister's paternal grandpa thought that I spent the money for his grandchildren. I felt sorry for my half-sister and half-brother, but who would feel sorry for me?

My maternal grandma arranged a schedule for my cousins and me everyday. My aunts and my mom had to work; my cousins and I had school all morning until 12:30 noon. We ate lunch at home and took an hour nap after lunch. Even though my cousins and I did not feel sleepy, we still had to sleep for an hour and that was grandma's rule. We were crying but after five or ten minutes, we felt into sleep because we were tired of crying. At first, I thought grandma should not force us to do what we did not want, but later I realized she helped us to stay healthy. we used to the schedule. Even though grandma was not saying anything, we still went to sleep as our habit. Grandma room was a medium master bedroom. The bedroom made with clean marble floor and warm ambiance. There was wide and high glass door before stepping out the balcony that made the room looked very antique. Each of us had a reserved place in grandma's room. We had to turn our face into the wall during sleeping and facing into the wall would help us distract the outside world and concentrate into our sleep. While we were sleeping grandpa usually opened the balcony door widely so we could inhale the fresh air completely. we rarely came into grandma's room without her permission. None of us, my cousins and I would have gut to step in grandma's room. We did not know where the feeling came from and why we were scared of her that much. Perhaps, she was a role model that we never wanted to be and the loving for her never existed in us. After an hour nap at noon, I did my homework at school and helped grandma prepared food for dinner. We usually ate dinner at 6:00PM. The television program started at 7:30PM and ended at 10:00PM everyday. We prayed after finishing the Television program. I always remembered the first words grandma started to pray. She called the Communist was an atheist. I never understood what she really meant at that time, but we prayed with her. Sometimes we were too tired and sleepy that we didn't want to pray and wanted to go to sleep early. Grandma wouldn't let any of us. She said the hell put its penis on our mouth. My cousin and I laughed so hard whenever we sat together and retold the memories about grandma. After two years I was in America, grandma was passed away after several long years suffering from diabetic and arthitis. I remembered it was beginning of June 1991 and that was the day I never forgot. There was the mix feeling inside me. I was sad to say that I wanted to see grandma died by my own eyes, but I didn't have a chance. I could not afford a ticket to Vietnam, but the actual reason was I also suffered through an emotional pain. I remembered grandma clearly; her cruel actions could never be counted. Now everybody mounted loving her. I hated myself so much for never forgiving grandma until the day I died because my soul remembered how I felt even if I forget what I felt.

My Bestfriends

Are you not ashamed of heaping up the greatest anount of money, honor, reputation, and caring so little about wisdom and truth and the greatest improvement of the soul?

Socrates

In three words I can sum up everything I've learned about life. It goes on.

Robert Frost

09

When I was fourteen years old, I lived near by a small catholic church that I used to sing in the choir there three days a week. I had three best friend names: ThuyMy, CamMy, and QuynhMy. They were all very talented, attractive single females, and specially very religious girls. Our houses were closed together and we used to go to the daily mass with each other at the church.

ThuyMy was the most attractive girl and older than me three years old, but she was a very stubborn, smart and spoil girl. Her house opened the tailoring business, but every time I went visiting her she dressed very funny and sexy. ThuyMy was just in a piece of silk cloth covering her body without any style. Her body was skinny and dark brown skin that made me felt vomit because she didn't have anything to wear at home. She didn't have a sexy body, but she had a pretty face like a victora secret suppermodel, "Tara Bank". ThuyMy could argue for her point very well. She said if we didn't come and bother her no one would see her in this cloth dress. Inside of her house, she had her own room; no one ever bothered her, so she didn't need to dress nice for any one to see. Plus, she didn't have any secret admirer or she didn't falling in love with anyone. ThuyMy talked a lot and could beat her enemy any time by just snapped her finger. However, she had never harm other people yet because she was also gentle and loving. Whatever I did wrong to her, she always protected me in front of people and tried to solve the problem with me later. That was what I liked about ThuyMy. One day I was dating the boy who was helping the priest during the mass. The priest terminated me out of the church. ThuyMy took me inside in front of the priest's room trying to argue for my right, but the priest was so stubborn that we had to follow his rule. He said I seduced one of the future priests and it was better for me to leave before other following my step. I did not know the boy will be the future priest and the boy left the church not because of me; he wanted to help his family financial support and he liked me. The priest was not being fair and he thought I was the problem. In fact, I liked the boy too but it seemed I had so much trouble when dated him. It was a big surprise to me, ThuyMy wrote in my memory book and gave to me as a souvenir when I was leaving for America, "I was not dating him, but it did not mean I was stopped loving him." ThuyMy was in the choir for almost ten years and I truly didn't know she had a crush on the same guy I dated. Later she was in America with her family and I accidentally met her in a night club. When I left Vietnam, we lost contacting with each other. Perhaps, I felt I owed her something which could not be repaid. I went to a Halloween party and Nick (my friend's friend) was there crazy for me. ThuyMy fell for Nick for so long but Nick ignored her since the day he saw me on that Halloween party. I didn't know how to call this situation, but ThuyMy thought I hated her and wanted to prevent. No matter how much I explained she didn't listen; she said I intended to repeat the tragic to make her jealous. I didn't want to make life complicate, but it repeated as the way it was without being plan for it. Again, ThuyMy wrote me a letter with a question I never forgot in my memory, "Why do you have to love the one I love for many years?" The problem was I didn't love. It just came and I was willing to sacrify my love for her, but she never know know much I appreciated her friendship to me when she tried to protect me even though it was not successful.

Another one of my bestfriend was CamMy. She looked innocent and everything in her life was simple. She seemed not worry anything at all. CamMy always dressed neat and nice. She had a rich and handsome boyfriend that swore to love her for the rest of his life. CamMy's family involved in black market that was why they were very rich and she never had to worry about money for her education and shopping. I didn't know it was faith or not but I never seen any happy life like CamMy, my best-friend. CamMy never had to worry about cooking, visiting her boyfriend, and making money. All she needed to do were eat, sleep, shopping and go to church. Her boyfriend even told me stopping her if she studied too much that would be not good for her health. It was different from me, nobody cared and responsible for me. In fact, CamMy was not a bad girl. She always loved me like a sister, but the love she had for me was not her responsibility. It was just a feeling of a bestfriend and she never knew how my maternal grandma behad to me. Her life was so fortunate and cheerful that she never knew tragic. Everytime we talked about distressing things that we experiented in our lives, she complained for being headache because she never coped with that in her life. Our purposes were to make her learn so she won't be afraid when she faced tragic, but she never wanted to know.

QuynhMy was the most prettiest and deep thought in one of my best-friends. She was my age and very gentle girl. QuynhMy and I were like blood-sister when my half-sister wasn't around me. QuynhMy wasn't have a father around her just liked me and a man who lived with her mom she did not really know the true history. However, he lived there loving her mom and took care of her. Somehow, QuynhMy found the man wasn't manly enough to handle a family and she wondered about the relationship between that man and her mom. Her mom was a strict woman; any time QuynhMy asked about that man, her mom was angry and said she was nosy. Same like me I didn't have a dad when I was friend with QuynhMy. That was why we got along very well. We revealed our secrets to each other. We always asked questions, but no one had answer to any of our questions. QuynhMy had a handsome boyfriend that loved her very much. However, that man was very sexual stimulated and cruel. He always wanted to have sex with her whenever we went to the movie together. She just wanted to satisfy him to keep their relationship smoothly. Eventually, each time she had sex with him, she turned out bruces all her body and blood came out from her vagina that hurted her badly. She decided to stop going out with him, but unlucky for her at that time she was pregnant. Again I had to leave to America and as I heard from ThuyMy that QuynhMy came back to that guy so the child has a father. QuynhMy died during her delivery the baby because her private part was infected and damaged badly that she must have a C-section. I was crying in the dark and hit myself for not being there with her because I knew I could comfort and advise her. Her mom never knew QuynhMy clearly after her dad left her mom because she lost and strict; QuynhMy wanted someone to be with when her loneliness striked her and I was always with her. However, each of us had our own life and I thought death was the way helping QuynghMy out of this brutal world. She died when she was eighteen years old.

Before I left QuynghMy, ThuyMy, and CamMy, we had unforgetable memory together. One day we were visiting the zoo on a tricycle. It was about ten miles from my house. After looking at the entire animal in the zoo; we were so hungry and decided to eat. There was a popular Vietnamese noodle soup that I loved so much. The noodle soup originated from the fartest south. It prepared with rice vermicelli, tomatoes, crab meat, and eat with spinach and a special shirmp sauce during the meal. we ordered three big bows and ate them all like pigs. Unfortunately, when we finished eating, we found out that our money was all gone. The money was dropped somewhere and I was the person who was in charged of all the money. I searched everywhere, but it was hopeless. My three bestfriends looked at me in fury eyes. I was trembling and lost. We were so scared and did not know what to do. I tried so hard to convince the owner that I would be back to pay for the meal and I meant it, but the owner kept laughing at my face. I was crying and begging him to grand me his generosity, but he just yelled out lout for people looking at us. I imagined that I could chop his mouth any minutes. I accepted my mistake for being careless about the money. I decided with my friends running away into the crowd while people around were busy eating, but the plan was not successful. We were not so lucky. One of the waiters caught us. The owner made four of us standing in front of the crowd. Thousand of the eyes were staring at us. They spat and swore at us like we had done a first degree murder. After three hours, the owner released us. We were so tired and had to walked ten miles home carrying the stiffy humilliation. I ever had that insulted experience in my life. My grandpa used to tell me, if I give my generosity to help people, my children or grandchildren will gain credits from the goodness that I have helped people. All those times I wonder what was my parent really did for me to gain this badly credit.

We were often together and thought of action to do. I went out with my friends to pick fruits because we didn't have money to buy fruits. A neighbor near by my house, she had a big garden with all the delicious fruits. There was a custard apple, one of my favorite fruit in her garden. The custard apple was also the only one on her tree. The tree was tall that I could not reach the fruit. My friends had to carry me on their shoulders so I could reach up to pick the custard apple. While I reached the fruit, the owner of the garden suddenly came out yelling out loud. She was about fifty years old widow and looked like a witch. My friends were so terrify of the widow's voice; They pushed me down the road and ran away so fast. I fell on the road with scatches all over my body. The angry widow hid me in a very dark storage for almost two daays without eating. The storage was an extremely stinky place and bugs flew all over my body. I was so exhausted when the widow released me. I went home with wonder why nobody cared for where I was. It liked a dream. All my best friends were scared too, but I told them not ever to tell anyone anything if I was in trouble. If I told my grandma, she probably yelled back at me for wandering on the street and did bad things. It was a big lesson for me to learn never wanting anything that didn't belong to me. Nothing is free in this world. If it is free, it is worthless.

My Half-Sister

I wore my half-sister sunglasses because I wanted to see and feel the durable darkness on her way in twenty years living without knowing who was her real blood father. She had an unbeatable heart for being strong and independent girl.

10

She was born after me almost three years. We grew up together, but we didn't share feeling until one day we realized that we had may things in common. When we came to America, we had times to be with each other and I felt closed to my half-sister more. We started to share feeling. My half-sister is a 5'4" twenty years old woman who looks average. Her father left when she was a baby. However, I thought my dad was much more generous than my half-sister's dad because at least my dad accepted her as a daughter, but her dad did not even realize one of his genes had fell off for all those actions that he had done to my mom. I was much luckier than my half-sister because at least I had chance to see my dad whether he was good or bad. My half-sister didn't know her real father was for twenty years already. No one knew where her dad was right now and nobody wanted to talk about her dad for it would remind my mom a sad memory. Life had put her in a difficult situation, but I never thought that faith was arranged for her. Her father made the decision not to see her and he could change that decision any time. He is a doctor; life of the people are in his hand; there are no faith. One could change faith, although he did not believe in faith. I loved her more than I loved my father. However, I was just a sister. I felt I closed to her more than I closed to my father. However, I seemed lucky than her at least I knew who my dad was. Sometimes, our thoughts were exactly the same that made us freak out. My half-sister is a very smart sister. My wish was someday, I could earn enough for her to continue her education. She worked and took care of herself very well, but she never had enough to support her education tuition. It wasn't my obligation to support her, but I felt useless to be her older sister and watched her education incompleted each day. I always felt bitterness around me. It was raining outside all day. I didn't like rain because sadness always happened in the raining days. The night my boyfriend's brother was together with my sister, it was scattering rain. All the raining days turned my life so badly.

I used to watch the rain through the window in happpy and told my cousin that he was crazy because he said rain was sad. Now I just afraid to see ton of water. Rain…Sea…Water…All of them related to depression. I often dreamed to have a house facing the beach so I could listen to the sea waves whispering, see the sun set, and hear the voice of the litte mermaid singing. Life is never a dream. Whatever rain brought to my life, I still didn't want my half-sister to get influent in it. Somehow, she did and I felt so guilty for all the actions I had put my half-sister through.

The first time my boyfriend visited me in California. We were so happy together. He went with his brother, Mike. Mike was a nice and successful young man. I wanted to spend all my times with my boyfriend and told my half-sister to tour Mike. Mike and my half-sister got along with each other very well and I fell happy for both of them at that time. Everything wasn't as the way I thought. After my boyfriend and his brother went back to their home, Florida. My half-sister was crying and notified me; Mike was a bastard. May be Mike didn't mean to hurt her and nobody is perfect. Either Mike or my haf-sister did not think well before they were together. They were all adults that could be able to think well for themselves. My half-sister was a strong girl, but love came from emotion. My half-sister never made anything important, but when she thought a matter was important; it must be serious. At least, Mike called and cleared out with her that he didn't like long distance relationship or he didn't think well on that one night stand with her. My half-sister was a faithful girl and she was being hurt. I felt bad because if Mike respected me he would not do such silly action. Mike promised to call my half-sister after that one night stand

and left her with hope. His action was not a mistake, but an animal action. I saw Mike's girlfriend with happiness in his apartment, but I still felt sorry for my sister even though my half-sister had a boyfriend too. I sat there seeing each of my sister dropping tears. Her saying was "I was with him because I wanted to forget my past. I didn't love him. Whatever he did to other, it will come back to him." I heard my boyfriend voice, "They were all adults. They knew what they were doing. It took two to Tango and nobody fault." What did I say? I was sitting on the balcony watching the dawn, crying with the cold fogg, and waiting for Mike's party to end so my boyfriend would come back. I wasn't sad because I couldn't go to the party. I was sad because nobody answered my questions, "Why didn't my boyfriend want me to go to Mike's party with him? His brother didn't want me to see his animal face? What did I do wrong? My boyfriend suspected that I would out of control to insult Mike during the party or Mike didn't want to remind him his animal action. After that incident, I felt I was using my half-sister like a one nightstand pitch in a game for my own good. That was why I wanted to wear her sun glasses so I could see the darkness that I had caused her to comfort her. She intended to lose the baby with Mike for her heart got stronger after the Tango night.

The New Land

"Keep ancient lands, your storied pomp!" Cried she
With silent lips. "Give me your tired, your pour,
Your huddled masses yearning to breathe free,
The wretch refuse of your teeming shore.
Send these, the homeless, tempest-tost to me,
I lift my lamp beside the golden door!"
Emma Lazarus

11

On the first day, America was so thrilling and exciting. I thought my life would be changed completely. It was true that my life had been changed. It had changed into a different life, a life with more distressing and sorrow. I could never forget that day in my life; my dad and I faced each other for the first time in fifteen years. I was in a great joy of tears, so did my dad. My dad reached his arms around my mom, my half-sister, my half-brother, and me and held us tightly. I questioned myself, "Why would I wanted to see the man that never be there with me when I needed him, the man seemed to forget his responsibility during I was in Vietnam, and the man never knew where my heart is. I looked at my dad strangely while tears came down my cheek. I whispered that I saw him because he was my dad, a man who gave his generous heart to my half-sister and my half-brother even though they were not part of his genes.

In the beginning, my family lived in an apartment near my paternal grandparent's house. My paternal grandpa died from cancer and I didn't know exactly what was the kind of cancer that he really suffered through. My dad and my paternal grandma told me that they had to pay a great deal of money for my paternal grandpa's sickness. During the time that my paternal grandpa was sick, all the family's members had to work so hard to support paternal grandpa's medical situation.

My paternal grandma had to work at her fifty five years of age. She had to take bus an hour from her house to her work place every day. At first, she washed dishes in a restaurant. Later, she learned how to cook so good that they accepted her as a chief cooker in that restaurant. My paternal grandma was a very gentle and nice woman. She always laughed, but I knew deep inside of her she felt much sorrow and lonely since my paternal grandpa passed away. Sometimes. I talked to her a lot about my personal life. She shared her experiences and advised me. I didn't live with her for long, but she was a very lovely grandma. My panernal grandma and maternal grandma had one thing in common that they both felt lost, pain, and lonely when their husbands passed away. They were both very emotional. The different between them was the mood and behavior. my paternal grandma was very calm woman and she never swore. My maternal grandma was a very cruel woman and swearing seemed to be her habit. Everytime I thought about dad, I thought of how nice my paternal grandma compared to my my maternal grandma. My thought was conflicted and I just realized personalities granted from nature.

I knew about my paternal grandma's personality after a year living in the apartment near her house in America. I noticed paternal grandma because her husband left just like my maternal grandma's situation. A year living in America, my mom carried another child who was my blood brother. When my blood brother was born, my family moved in with paternal grandma. I think we moved because our family financial was too tight. My dad never revealed his feeling, but I could see the worry in his eyes. Everyday, he gave my half-sister and me, each of us two dollars fee. He also bought a monthly bus pass for each of us to take bus to school. Sometimes, he had to borrow one of my aunts' money for the basic expense in the house. He was unemployed and the General Aid was not enough for the family. My mom was on welfare. I was very sad to say that I was too young to help. I remembered when my family lived in Oakland, we had an old car, and I did not recover what was the car's brand name. One day, my dad drove us to visit my paternal grandma. On the curve turned to the freeway, the car stopped running and my family had to walk about five miles home. Well, we walked home in half happiness and half difficulty. At that time, my dad was a smoker. He could smoke two packs of cigarette a day. Sometimes, I saw him smoking continuously beside his bed and my mom was pregnant lying on the other side of the bed. Dad told his friends that smoking released his sadness. I think he just wanted to get away from the truth, the truth was my mom, and he did not expect the baby coming. Seeing lack of financial need, I usually got mad at my mom for being pregnant in the wrong time even though it was not her fault. I felt bad when mom cried, but her weakness was never surprised me. I was too young to help my parent accept trying to study hard. However, being poor never stopped us to go on with our life ahead. My family still hoped for the future.

School in America

My family moved places to places and I had to move high school to high school. Oakland Technical was the first high school I attended since my family lived in America, but I graduated from other High School, San Learndro. My true dream was to become a nurse someday. When I was ten years old, I was in the hospital for appendix remover. The nurse who took care of me during I was in bed was my mom. Her excellent care never stopped my dream to become a nurse since then. Whenever I thought of all the helpful and generous that my mom gave people, I forced myself to study hard and put all my effort in school each day. However, being a foreign student in American high school often terrified me. The majority of students in High School were black. The minority was Asian. I never meant to discriminate between colors, but I always had trouble with those black students around me when I was in high school. I did not speak English that well; that was why I never be friend or speak to them. I never tried to bother those black students, but most of the time they teased my friends and me for being immigrants taking their spaces in America. I thought about they never meant what they said, perhaps, they just being jealous to all the successful immigrants in American land. America was their motherland and their achievement was only little compared to the Asian because they, themselves, were also the majority in their motherland compared to the white population. At that time, I did not care that much when those black students teased me because I did not understand their language that much somehow. Unfortunately, they started to notice my weakness in commnicating their language. They thought about another way to oppress my friends and me. They became very cruel and acted like lunatic. They liked to chase my friends and I liked "Tom and Cherry" in the cartoon character that I usually loved to watch. Now I was filled with terror when I figured out I was in the same situation like Jerry. We ran around the school and when we were tired, we stopped to confront their massie bodies. One of the black girls pushed me down the school grasses and said, "Ya fool small eyes get back to your country. How can you see when the blackboard is too small and dark in your eyes, huh. Yellow is not belong here." At that time I did not understand what the black girl said, but each of her words recorded clearly in my memory. I did not know what to say when I began to understand those words. Well, America still had justice that was why I survived to know there was bad and good people in this society.

At another time, those black students chased us again; my friends and I were running like crazy. Ahead of us, a spiky thorn fence stopped us from running. We were scared to death, but still got the strength to climb over the other side of the fence. My mind was blank at that time. Scratches with blood were all over my body, which resulted from those spiky thorns on the the fence. My friends and I were suffering and frightening, but what should we do? Nobody would dare to report to the principle in school because we were anxious. If those black students got punished, we would get prevent from them as well. They looked like the hungry tigers that could kill us anytime. People wished to stay in school to finish their dream, but I hoped I could get out of school as soon as possible. I could be died before trying to accomplish my dream. I often looked at those black students inside filled with fury and sorry for myself.

After two years, my family moved in with my paternal grandma and I transferred to a new high school. This school was more surprised to me than ever because this time the majority of the students in school was white. They were more civilized and mushy. They didn't hurt people by physical strength, but they hurt people by words because they were much smarter than those black students. They defeated people by their language and I believed that was the fair way to survive in this society. I had to challenge myself into another world. Most of the times I used my hands or made face expression to help my teachers helping me. I had a very hard time in school, but my spirit never let me stopped going to the future of my dream. As the only Vietnamese girl among uncounted white girls, I began to understand the experiences of isolation, helpless, and rage regularly reported by minority students. I had no friends, but luckily, all the courses that I took in school were those courses I already learned in my country, Vietnam. I learned English when I was ten years old. At the time, I was learning English; I did not dedicate myself into it that much. One of my aunts was a good English teacher and she always forced me to study. I often thought my aunt was crazy because people didn't speak to each other in English in Vietnam. Now, I thanked my aunt so much and it was my big mistake if I did not listen to her. I graduated from the new School with a pleasing GPA. 3.87 at early eleven grade because I had enough credits.

My dad found a job in Sacramento and my family moved again. Sacramento is a very small and peaful city, but it has a very hot weather. When it was hot, it was obove hundred degrees hot. Most of American did not like this kind of dry weather. I quickly adapted to the weather because I was used to the tropical weather in Vietnam. However, I sometimes experienced the migrain headache inherried from the hot weather. I continued my education by attending in a community college near my house. It was a small and peaceful school. I especially liked the school's ambiance. After my classes, I usually sat on the green grasses under a big marble tree in the center of the school. The view of the falling leaves reminded me the long road full of tamarind leaves when I was the schoolgirl in Vietnam. The falling Tamarind leaves and I were in the same path. The leaves tasted bitter like my life. The day I was noticing those leaves falling slowly, it was the day I knew my hope in becoming a nurse was an illusion. Whenever I weeped bitterly, I knew things would be happened unaware. I did not know the unaware was faith or not, but I could feel my lost of energy each day as I went to school and from that day I knew I would be gone like the falling leave.

After a year in college, I had a serious surgery on the back of my neck. The pain receiving from the surgery had stopped me from going to school for almost two years. However, sickness never left me me alone. I went back to school carrying another sickness, Seizure. I did not know the seizure was resulted from the surgery or not, but it affected my life badly. The hospital and the school reported to my family more often about my seizure accidents. My doctor advised me not to think hard and use my memory that much. I wasn't a smart girl, how could I stop study hard for my future? I could not drive because I may harm other people during my driving. If a person died, I would feel regret for all my life for intend to kill. I was collapsed and dropped out of school. I tried and tried so hard for my dream, but I could not concentrate at all. I felt embarrass with my half-sister because we was often talking about she would become a doctor and I would become a nurse to help her open a charity hospital in Vietnam. I was completely downhearted. They even resisted me when I tried to joint the Peace Corp. From a confident girl, I became a loser. Whenever I went out with my parent, I weep after I went home because their friends had the better children to brag about. My parent did not say anything, but I knew they were helpless to have a surviving creature in their life that they had to accept as a burden because they created this unwanted creature. I loved school. Since I was the first grade to twelve grade student, I always was the best in class. Life seemed never smooth and fair as the way I wanted to be. I entered community college as many other students to complete my dream. I loved philosophy because I thought life was an obstacle that I never stopped to learn, to observe, and to express the boundary of life.

I never thought the word "white teacher" would be appropriated, but I just meant to describe the detail. In one of my English classes, I had a white English teacher in Community college. I never meant to be raced between color and impolited to my teacher. I was the only one Asian student in this English class. The teacher had never seemed to satisfy of my works. She always criticized heavily on all my essays. My dad usualy said if someone still concerned about me they always commented about me; I agreed with dad. One day the teacher called me up to her office and gave me a long lecture about I should not talking this English 1A class. I said this English 1A was General Education requirement; If I wasn't taking this course I didn't know my English was weak. Her job was to teach and help me to pass the class for my future purpose, not to tell me which course should or should not take. She was discouraging me. After talking to my English teacher, I felt shattered and was about to quit the class. Thinking about the final grade, I changed my mind. The final exam was fifty percent of the overall grade. I needed to pass the final exam in order to pass the English class, I took my sister "A" grade essay and turned in as my final exam essay. However, the teacher gave me a D grade and commented I had very bad English, but she did not correct any gramma or spelling in my essay. I didn't know what to do. I couldn't speak English well enough to argue against her. I went straight to my English teacher honestly said it was not my essay. She stood in front of the class shouting at me and trying to insult me. All the students in class were staring at me. My Engligh was not good enough to defeat my teacher, but I wanted to chop her evil face into pieces. She glanced at me laughing as a winner had completely defeated her enemy in front of the soldiers. I accepted an F for cheating, but she was insulting my sister's teacher as well. We did the same topic on an argumentative essay. At least, my teacher gave me a passing grage. She supposed to feel wrong for the reason of not grading carefully. I was about to tell my sister what was really happened, but I took my half-sister essay without her permission. I thought about those teachers who graded students' essays in school everyday. Did they ever make mistakes? Was my grading essay a mistake or a devastating result for cheating? From an A grade essay to a failing essay in the same topic, who had the wrong teacher? After this experience, I had the fear of being around any white American teacher. Everytime they were around me I had the nervous feeling and imagined their defeating laughs that could kill me anytime on American land. Well, there must be some of them good too, but I thought I was not lucky enough to know any of them.

People took four years to graduate from college. I spent seven years reaching to my dream as a nurse. Had I achieved anything? No, I had ended nowhere. I had to take the state board exam in order to be a registered nurse. What was the use when I became one? Would they let me care for the patients when I had seizure? Was America a dream land or a disaster land? Why I had to live in this land when one of my uncle said my life would not go any further and I had to settle down with a man in order to grow up? I came to this land for my sister's boyfriend called me an empty head? They did not respect me at all, because they knew I was useless and helpless to survive by myself. Was it my fault to become sick? Did I come to this land to see my family breaking into pieces? Did I come to this land to experience the pain of a loser? Did I come to this land to hear my boyfriend said he could not marry me because I could not bare children? Life was fair, was it? There must be a winner along with a loser and "The winner takes it all" (ABBA).

The Lovers

We were strangers, starting out on a journey,
never dreaming, what we would have to go through.
Now here we are, I am suddenly standing
at the beginning with you,
No one told me, I was going to find you.
Unexpected, what you did to my heart.
When i lost hope,
You were there to remind me.
And life is a road and i wanna keep going
Love is a river, i wanna keep flowing
Life is a road now and forever-wonderful journey
I'll be there when the world stops turning
I'll be there when the storm is through…
Nothing is going to tear us apart.
Donna Lewis & Richard Marx

12

How much I knew about Georgia? I knew it much more than I imagined. The interview with the Airline was not a successful one, but through this interview's trip I learned and realized many tragics in this life. I supposed to reserve a hotel room, but one of my bestfriends said it was safer to stay at her fiance's house in Marietta, Georgia. My bestfriend's fiance lived in an apartment with his aunt and on that day, his aunt went away on vacation. I had a choice to stay in his aunt's room. I wanted to save money, but it turned out I saved to damage myself. In the middle of the night, my bestfriend's fiance had a fit of sexual stimulated. He came in his aunt's room and lay next to me on his aunt's bed. I asked out loud, "What are you doing in here? Something to tell me?" I had sensed something wrong will happen and I was right. He tried to wrap me, but I already prepared for his low action. I wrapped my purse and ran out the street heading to the apartment next door.

I knocked the near by apartment's door and yelled so hard for help. A big tall mexican man opened the door and let me in his apartment. He looked very nice and tall. I sat on his sofa crying and trembling in fear. The Mexican man gave me a big blanblet and calmed me down. However, I was wrong about this man because this time I destroyed myself for trusting people. While the Mexican man tried to comforted me, I laid my head on his shoulder. Unfortunately, he wrapped his arms around my body tightly and pushed me down the sofa. He sealed my mouth by a strong and sticky tape. He used all his strength pushing me down the sofa; I could not move or speak and fainted after a while exhaused with striking. When I woke up, I did not see the Mexican man. It was blood all over my body and I was hurt to death. I ran out the street with pain and bruises all over the body with the empty mind. My clothes were tearing up and I was like a beggar on the street did not know what to do and whom should I ask for help. I remembered sitting in the corner of the cross street and it was scattering rain out side. I did not know I was crying or drops of rain fell on my cheek, but I thought my life was over from that day on. The water poured into my mouth and tasted so bitter. I closed my eyes and tried to bite my tougue ending up my life. Suddenly, a very elegant and beautiful lady about forty years of age drove a black Mercede came close to me and said, "Oh! Poor girl. What happened to a pretty girl like you? Come into my car. I will help you the best I can." I could not guess her nationality through her accent or her look. I just stepped on her car thinking about my shelter first. The woman lead me to a white mansion standing in the middle of a big field with all those marble trees around the mansion. Inside the mansion, it decorated like a nightclub with dim lights everywhere but every romantic enviroment. I guessed It was a high-class nighclub and it was true. I stayed in a big a big room with all the necessities in two day. No one bothered me until the third day, the elegant woman came in, and told me to dress up because I had a job needed to be done tonight. She said, "If you want to get home quickly, just do what I say tonight and tomorrow you will be home safe." I heard my dad's voice close to my ear that in a precarious situation, I had to act under circumstances. That was the only way I could help myself. I hosted a man that night as requested and used the share of money to go home. The woman used me to get money and I used the sharing part of money getting home. I came home, but I felt my body was somewhere else. Nobody asked where I was, but it was okay for me without asking from anyone. People needed not to know because I was not who I wanted to be anymore. I felt like a savage; even though all the experiences were unexpected. Georgia was my hatred, my nightmare, and more than that it put me in a tragic. Would my bestfriend going to believe her fiance was a bastard? I always wished to be a virgin, but what a virgin did to help herself out of danger? Did the mermaid gain anything when she was in love deeply with the prince? I used to think I was a trash that no man would want; trash would always have a chance to recycle. Sometimes the leaves fell not because the season, but the dirt sticked on them was too heavy. I became a player and found out that I didn't have to be pretty in order to become a player. After the experience in Georgia, I dated many men at once without being afraid. I just wanted to play around, made men crazy about me, and dumped them to release my anger. For almost three years, I partied and came home late at night. I knew it was very dangerous for a girl to go out until 3:00AM but I was not myself anymore. I did not care about what my dad advised, but was stubbornly angry againsted him. I liked to date marrying men. They spoiled me as their lover and I enjoyed being their lover. A lover did not have many obligations like a wife and men usually did not expect much from their lover. I even went out with a Mafia. He came from Switzerland and was very rich. He spoiled me and gave me money to play stocks. I didn't know anything about stocks and I lost but that didn't hurt me because it was not my money. Later the Mafia's wife found out I hang around with her husband and almost killed me. That night, I was so scare because she stabbed on my arm with a sharp knife, but she was not success. I stopped dating that Mafia man. There was a fifty years old man asking me to marry him in a nightclub and I accepted. I wanted to surprise my family by did not tell them that a fifty years old man came to propose to me. I thought I could make life simple for me by settle down this way. Unfortunately, on the way he came to proprose to me he got into the accident and died without saying goodbye. I didn't feel sad that much because I did not love him. He wanted me and I gave him a chance to have me. I always thought about the bitter life and somehow it was true for people who was born in the year of the tiger. After the fifty years old man death, I inherrited a million dollar from his account, but his mother behaved to me like a bitch. She said I only wanted his money. The truth was I did not love him but I also did not know about his wills. I threw the money on his mother's face and ran away from her evil face. I did not attend his funeral. Sometimes, a person had to be a pitch in order to survive, but I did not survive through that thought. I felt sorry for myself and life was not easy like I thought it was. I played bad because I thought I could prevent life. All I had been through was just harmed myself and lost my value each day. I looked back and realized that seeing my dad cold and grouchy face was better than going out seeing those dating man. Once my dad told me it was never too late to learn. I just followed my heart and I would be fined.

I came back to school to continue my nursing major. One day I met a neurologist. He worked in a private clinic. I told him my dream to be a nurse and he promised to help me on my dream. I used to come to his clinic for a visit with a few question regarded to my medical situation. Sometimes I brought him lunch to appreciate his guidance. One day the neurologist's wife saw I was talking with her husband in the private room at the clinic. She suspected that I had affair with her husband. I knew the complication would happen. I felt tired and bored. I didn't know what to think and what to do anymore. I stopped going to school in depression.

I again became wild. I started to drink and smoke to forget my life. I borrowed the bitter of wine to distract the sorrow in the heart. I could feel that I forgot everything when I was drunk. Lovers, problems in family, and in school, I did not feel any of that interesting than drinking and dancing in the nightclub. One day, I was in the nightclub I felt nausea in my burning stomach for drinking too much. A woman brought me home and took care of me. She advised that a young girl like me had a bright future ahead, why did I put myself down in darkness. I should not give up because living in this life I had to struggle and to challenge myself. She said she would contact one of her friends to offer me a job. Her friend was a loan officer and also a broker. The broker needed a personal secretary. I was hesitated because I was afraid of being next to a man for the mistake I had been through. I told the woman I thought about going back to school. She said I just took time and let her know when I was ready.

In two weeks, I noticed the woman's husband. He was a rich young man mingled with his handsome face. He seldom talked, loved his children a lot and very calm with his wife. With his characteristics many women would dream to have a gentlement like him. I wouldn't dare because his wife helped me so much on the way with all her generosity. One day, I had tea with the woman's family including her husband in the back yard. Her husband looked at me strangely and said he had a job for me. I felt so happy that night and could not sleep. My job was going out with him and did secretary jobs that he asssigned. That evening, a designer came designing my own evening gown to the dinner party with him. He glanced his dearest romantic hazel eyes at me said I was beautiful in that designing dress and he would not surprise if any men fell crazily for me. I was stunt to hear his voice because he never flirted. I answered back, "How much do you love me if I give you all my passion?" He left without any reply. I did not that was love or not but I felt safe and happy when I was with him. He was everything I wished I would have. My heart delighted when I heard that he chose me to go out with him because his wife was pregnant. I didn't feel my job there was appropriated anymore. I decided to leave and accepted the job that the woman reffered me to her friend before. I never forgot her husband sad lovely eye looking at me at the airport, but he didn't said any words to me. What could he say? He knew that I fell for him and nothing would change the way he was now. I just didn't want to involve in anybody family. He was a young successful man with a good heart. I heard about his happily background with his family, but I never cared about that. All I remembered was his deep voice, gentleness, and quietness. His family lived in Los Angeles, but later they moved to New York. The husband usually travelled around and stopped by visiting me. I had dinner with him couple of times, but the last time I resisted because I told him I had a lover. The truth was I loved his image, the perfect lover that I could never find in my life. I started to worked for the broker, but my job was more than secretary. He asked me to buy even condoms and his underwears. I didn't care because buying those wasn't a hard job and as long as he paid me. Sometimes, he was so drunk and held me sitting on his lab. He laughed and said, "Honey! Be my lover." In fact, he was a fool and I just ignored him. He was drunk most of the times in the office and I started to feel weary. I began to have a serious migrain headache. The headache drove me crazy and I didn't know what caused it even the doctor. I hitted my head on the wall trying to release the pain and almost killed mytself. I still struggled with life each day I felt I had nothing but sorrow and confusion. Something in my life must be missing, but I hadn't not known. I tried to retrieve myself but nothing got me away from sadness. I was in front of the computer everyday waiting for the time went by so I could forget myself. Nobody asked me what I wanted, my habits, my soul, and what really went wrong in my life? The useless heart didn't know the destination of life. I found a replacement since I left that perfect gentlemnent throught internet. Benny, a man I ever loved, my boyfriend. He had changed my life completely. He talked to my heart and soul like a psychic. The first time I had ever in love with a man. Was this true love? Only time could answer.

The broker that I worked for; I told him how much I was in love with Benny, my boyfriend. The broker didn't notice what I revealed to him because my love was a long distance relationship. One day, the broker got into a serious accident. He died in the hospital because he lost quite a large amount of blood during the accident. I was beside him holding his hands. He tightened my hands and said he never forgave Benny for taking his girl away. He closed his eyes, but his fingers wrapped around my wrist tightly. I tried so hard to loosen his hands and went home with sympathy. I cleaned up his office, but had no idea where was his family or relatives. This was the first time, I read a diary of a man who had a crush on me. Even though he said he loved me, I didn't have any feeling for him and never would. I told Benny about the incident that happenned and was about to give the broker's diary for Benny to read. I suddenly undestood deeply the feeling of losing someone that I loved for all my heart. Benny never let me read the diary his feeling for his ex-lover. Even though I promised to Benny that I would give him the diary to read. Finally, I broke my promise to avoid whatever would cause even though I felt guilty for changing my mind so quickly. Benny and his ex-girlfriend loved each other for seven years and she left him a week just before the wedding day without any explaination. Many time Benny insisted me to give the broker's diary for him to read but I referred not to because I realized why he didn't give me the diary about his ex-lover to read even though I negotiated with him I would give mine. However, Benny and my relationship wasn't last for long for some reasons.

My Boyfriend

I was experienced the drizzle rain when my boyfriend told me we had no future together. The day I left Vietnam, it was sudden and short shower. The day my maternal grandma told me how ugly I looked, it was thunder rain. The day one of my bestfriend died, it was heavy rain. And the day I ran away from home, it was torrent rain. I was just afraid to see rain, water, and the sea. It always was a sign of sadness when I saw rain. My boyfriend loved to see the sea because it comforted his sadness; It was different from me. Sometimes you wanted to be something that you never wanted, but it just happened. Each person had their own emotion and behavior. That was how I loved my boyfriend despite the separation between our relationship. He was special than any other man, but how the relationship went wrong?

14

In a love relationship, there are three things that makes two heart together and last forever. Those are love, sex, and responsibility. I don't think any couple would last without any of that. My parent had sex and responsibility, but I don't think they have enough love for each other after sixteen years separated to lead them on. They stayed together because only of their responsibilities that was why they never got along with each other. My boyfriend and I love each other deeply. I love him and make love to him since the first day I was being with him. However, why do I always thinking that he is not a man with responsibility and I hide the true emotional distress inside of me? I ask myself is it true when people say love is just not enough. Why we love each other so much but why our relationship still went wrong? I bummed on Benny not on the street, but on the internet and we shared feeling to each other. We started to have a long distance relationship, but no one ever stopped me from loving him. Many times, I was lonely sitting on the dark missing him and weeping like a child. I didn't date other men because I just wanted to be faithful to him. I wanted to show him I wasn't the one before anymore and would die for him. I knew in his heart he also experienced the stressful emotion without my attendant. Whenever I was being with him, his hospitality and romance showed that I was special. He said he resisted other women because he wanted his heart put in my heart. However, if I wa a man, I probably knew the situation between us and figured out exactly what to do. In a relationship there was not just roman. A real man had to do what he had to do without hearing other tell him right and wrong. What do I mean by that?

Benny, my boyfriend, his name goes well with his handsome face and his athletic body make me hungry for him all the times. He said when I looked at him outside, he may look heartless, and strick, but inside of him there was love, gentle, and romantic emotion although he not expressed. Did those characters in him make he understood me more? Or Could he defind where my heart goes? May be the financial problem stopped him from seeing me, but he made our love more considerated. He wanted everything to be really for me and his when we marry, but how can it ready when he does not have a job or looking for one? As I saw he just stays home all day and uses the money that he gains from the stock market. That's when he wins; what's about when he loses? I don't think he can depend on the stocks for his living without a backup job. How can I persuade a stubborn man like him? He told me, "I would never listen to a woman. Don't waste your time to lecture or tutor me. I am not other and I do what I want to do. Woman can't involve in a man job." I guessed staying home unemployed and depending on stock was what he wanted to do. He forgot that beside him there was a woman that loved him and worried about him. Unless he just wantd to be with that woman when he felt love and lelf her alone when he couln't afford her. He just wanted to go his way and didn't care about the future being with me. Many times I felt sorry for a woman like me could'n tell my true disagreement to my boyfriend. I felt I was dishonest and useless just because I loved him so bad and didn't want to lose him. Did Benny have a heart to feel my grieve, not just love? Did he have responsibility of a man? or he always thought we were two people tango with each other like his brother did to my half-sister. He said after the one night-stand between his brother and my half-sister, "It takes two to tango and after that one night-stand, no one has to responsible for anyone" I was afraid of his statement because one day he may getting bored of our relationship and say the same. I dated a man who was tango with me for four years, but he never thought of propose to me; I am afraid that some day his observence will happen the same like the action between his brother and my half-sister and who am I going to rely on when he's leaving me with a pain heart because of loving him too deep. His saying made me insecured and may be just like his brother he would leave a sick girl like me. I knew Benny whatever he said he will do it. He never broke any promises. In my thought I am different from other normal girl because he had more hospitality and love over me. Would you want to be a special girl with no future with a guy? Benny never realized that I was different from other not just my sickness, but I also needed his help to get me out of my family's problems so I could start an independent life. I just wanted to be legally with him so I could have a reason for my parent let me out of the house happily. According to my family tradition, it was a shame for a girl to leave a house and lived illegally with a guy. I don't want to repeat the same problem like my mom did. I don't want my parent to worry about me when I get out off the house. If Benny loves me, he would help me and believe in my future. I don't need him to feed or worry for my living life. I just need his proper name to be my husband. However, my family let me go with him because they are tired of advising me. I run to him for help, he just denies me for the reason that he needs help himself. I was in between with sadness no one understands my situation. I want to look up, but no one trusts me and believes in me. They think I'm sick and useless. I am thinking, "what a boyfriend for when you need him and he has no trust in you? "

Benny and I lied to each other since the day we talked on internet. When he saw me, his expectation was changed and I experienced the hurtful and the true feeling from him. On the internet, he said he was studying Medical and I pretented to be a nurse to make our relationship go on smoothly as I love him. I guessed each of us having hope from each other. I had hope that I would get help from him as he will be a future medical doctor and he got hope for someday he will receive a caring and he won't have much responsible for me. It turned out to be different because we were both could not make our future career through as we wish. We both have problems of family, and personal that destroyed our concentrated mind. However, he made it through as a broker, the one he used to against it. I made it through as an interior design, but my career lead to no where because of my sickness, Seizure. The doctor advised me don't drive, and my driver lisence was suspended. I thought my boyfriend could help me going through the sickness by take over the responsibility for my parent. Being in America not driving could stop you from many things. My boyfriend just thought I am a burden and resisted the responsibility by telling me himself also need help. If my boyfriend knew his ability, he would never afraid of my situation and never spoke to me the hurtful words like he never thought to have future with me because of my Seizure and I could not bare children for him. After hearing his reason, I was downheart thinking that It was me who giving him too much responsibility, I don't deserve him. My heart was set in a wrong heart and It was my fault to choose his place. I still accepted to be his lover by hiding my feeling inside. I hope someday my feeling would change and may be he wasn't intended to hurt me. His word may not clearly enough to show love on the first day. A love feeling was very hard to find and I just needed times when he understood me enough to express his sorry. However, four years had passed even though he loves me deeply and dearly, but we didn't belong to each other. I always remembered the last time I cried inside his bed with him, but I was loving him and held him tight hoping for our relationship go on. I never felt so good yet felt so bad when knew our love would end someday. He was the only one I love, but I told him I didn't love him trying to let him go. I wanted to let him know that even though I'm not with him, I needed him so, but he left with his love for me. Leaving him wasn't easy, so many night I sufffered of missing him because to be out of his life I could not be free. I didn't need to touch him to feel him. I just couldn't get him out of my mind. We did tried to be together and all I wished that he would have a feeling that he needed me. However, he just the way he was, being alone and afraid to responsible for me. I was a love fool letting my heart aching. I felt sorry for myself that I should stop in the beginning so I didn't feel lost and dull in weakness of loving him. I thought I could change him, but I realized only he could change himself and I was wrong to have a hope like that. I remembered a lovely song of Babara Streisand, "Life is a moment to spare when a dream is gone, it's a lonely of place. I kiss the morning goodbye but down inside we know we never know why. The road is narrow and long when eyes meet eyes and the feeling is strong. I turn away from the wall; I stumble and fall, but I give you it all"

I went visit my boyfriend in Florida for two weeks. He spoiled me that I was getting lazy. Benny cooked, did the laundry, cleaning, took me to the most romantic and expensive restaurant, and I didn't have to spend a cent on anything. I loved him not because he spoiled me. It was because he was so gentle, patient, and lovely. I started to obsess with him that I became crazy and wanted to marry him. It seemed like he never wanted that way. In four years knowing him, I didn't know what did he really do for living. I saw him staying home most of the time and I felt worry when spending his money. He never wanted to tell me how he could afford all his personal stuffs even though I wondered. I felt he and I were closed enough to know his personal life, but he didn't say or care so. I didn't know what he felt about me but I felt I was a pitch who came to satisfy his desire and then left when he paid me. I wanted to be part of his life and showed my concern for him. I wanted him to take me out of my stressful living and to be with him. I wanted he and me to start our own life. Many couple begin from nothing achiving many supper circumstances in their life as long as they never give up the difficult situation. Benny never realized that to achive any difficulty, I needed his help. Even though I'm sick, but I never give up in anything and still have hope in myself. All I just need is some help from someone. My family and relatives got sick of me and they always think I am disable. Benny thinks it's too much responsibility for him to have me and he's afraid to face the reality of helping me. He gave me money to do things for my own . I wish I can express all my feeling of needing him, but the way he acts telling me that he can't handle the truth of loving me. Perhaps, I am not lucky like other girls and I'm also luckier than other girls because I am going out with an unresponsible man and experiencing the painful situation which not many girls experience through.

After the trip visiting Benny on the east coast, I went home with disappointment because I was having seizure and didn't have time to tell what I planned to tell before the trip. My sister said, "You're stubborn and crazy. You left your job going to him and when he was tired of you, he sent you home. You lost your job and can't pay for your bills. You can't doing like all the time; you have to get a life and settle in one place in order to build up a living." I don't know what Benny thinks. I better let him thinks of what to do than tell him doing what he never thinks he will do. I wish he hears what my sister had told me. However, I just think if he hears, will things going to change? or he keeps hanging me around so I get thirsty for more! Perhaps that the way Benny was.

The Journal to Vietnam

If my Dad wasn't financially support me, I wouldn't have a chance to go back to my mother country where I spent almost my childhood life over there. To me it was ten years since the day I left Vietnam, but to my Dad, it was twenty five years. My family started the trip in San Francisco Airport by Eva Airlines. On the plane I had a strange feeling of half-sadness and half-happiness. Ten years ago living in a dysfunctional family and society, I always wanted to get out of that world. Now I wanted to see it again so bad because all that memories reminded me how I grew up to be a decent woman.

There were two of my Dad's friends went along with my family. One was an engineer and one was a lawyer. Their friendliness made everybody felt easy and fun to be with. The weather made me exhaused all the time; not like ten years ago I lived in it. I was always tired and sweat all over my forehead. Vietnam ten years ago wasn't Vietnam today anymore. I was stunt to see all the changes. The city, Saigon was crowed with motocycles. The air was poluted by all the smoke from the moto-vehicles and dirt in the air. People didn't drive bicycles often like before I was there anymore unless those very poor people like students. All the people wore bands on their head to avoid breathing dirt from the air. The band covered all over their face and they wore sun glasses too. I wondered if they could see anything.

Many buildings and houses were built. The street was always busy and all vehicles only went about ten miles an hour; they always horned to each other even for nothing. The streets was no control. People drove all over to the directions that they wanted and didn't worry that they were in the wrong ways. I was scare at first, but I got adapted for a week. Still I couldn't stop my tearshread for those children begged on the streets. Some of them their parents forced to beg because people usually gave money for the kids than an adult. I didn't know I should laugh or cry when I gave a beggar one dollar, he turned his back without saying thank you and said, "You from America, why you are so cheap." He thought I could pick the money on tree in America. I was unemployed and my dad gave me one hundred dollar to spend, but I couldn't count all the beggars on the street in one city. My dad he had to pay a fee for the horse before he could sit on it taking pictures. Or else they would beat him up and those people that he paid not even the horse owners. I didn't feel right when sit on a high class restaurant and see all the beggars on the streets. What could I do? I couldn't afford all of them. What else could I do? Crying for being a useless and hopeless!

Ten years ago, one of my aunts used to babysit me when my mom was busy. She just liked my second mom and I loved her like a mother. Now, she was married and had two kid, but the house that she lived in was just a size of my bedroom (about two hundreds square feet) in America. Her husband was having three kids with another woman before marrying her. Every people hated him because he was lazy. He didn't want to do anything accept sitting around and being drunk all the time. He quitted after a short time to any job that my cousin referred him to; People who hired him said that they just respected my cousin, but they could stand a drunking man any longer. My aunt got supported from some of my aunts in America, but she gave her husband and he just spent all the money without thinking that he had two kids. My aunt didn't say anything because she was afraid her husband would beat her anytime if she againsted him and if she died no one would take care of her kids. She couldn't find a job because she had to take care of her sons, one was two and one was three years old. She couldn't afford a babysitter to go to work. The money that she had to pay for the babysitter was equal the money that she earned in one months. She thought It better for her to take care the kids, but she was poor. My other aunts stopped supporting her because they wanted her husband to know his responsibility to work. People only helped her when she helped herself; they couldn't help anyone just sitting there waiting for money to come. I felt sorry for my aunt, but nothing I could do to help her because she had chosen her own life even though people stopped her before marrying her husband. Everybody had their own problem. Even though the man I loved was nearly perfect, but I was still deep in sadness. I realized that only you could make your life better and never gave up on anything, there was no faith or destiny.

I visited the school where I used to attend when I was in junior high school. I studied there for nine years from first grade to nine grade. Now after ten years, it was still the same standing there reserved its antique. I went on the street with all the Tamarind leaves falling, the convent was still standing there in silent, romance, unique, beauty, and unforgetable memories. I was deep in sadness seeing the man used to be my date sitting one the side of the street waited for people to come by preparing motocycles. I didn't come to say hello because I was afraid he would be ambarrssed to see me. My thought was that he would feel uneasy with the imagination if I marry him, I probably have no future right now. I just stood on the other side of the street watching my old date without letting him know. My cousins said I was mean, but I rather be mean than making a man ambarass. I tried to give him some money, but I thought he would not accept. I remembered the old day I was with him; he used to tell me a story about there was a farmer. One day he found a big and precious diamond on his yard, but he was afraid robber would come killing him for the diamond. He tried to give the diamond to the king and said, " Robbers would not dare to come to your castle for the diamond, but they would come to me anytime for I'm a poor farmer without security." The king didn't accept the gift and said, "You think the diamond is precious, but I think my pride is precious. If I accept your diamond, we both lose our precious thing. Why don't you just keep yours and I keep mine; each person still has their own precious thing that was the best way okay." The farmer begged the king and said, "If I keep mine, the robber will come and harm me to get it any time, Please accept it" The king thought for a while. He brought the diamond to a jewelry shop and sold it. After that the king gave the money to the farmer so the farmer could buy more land to work and become rich. I thought my date's purpose wanted to tell me that his pride is precious and don't attempt to take away from his.

My dad rented a three story house. It was a nice and clean house with living room and kitchen. My dad and mom stayed in one room on the third floor and my little brother and I stayed in the room across my parent's room. The engineer and the lawyer stayed in the second floor and each of them had their own room. We had a lot of fun times together. My cousins usually stopped by talking to the engineer and the lawyer even though they didn't make sense, but they tried to learn. The engineer liked to learn Vietnamese and my cousins tried to learn English. They taught each other, but the lawyer didn't want to learn. I guessed he had too much pride in him although he is nice too. The engineer was very lovely and always smile. He was very patient and understandable. Even though the conversation between him and my cousins seemed difficult, he always kindly talked to them and never gave up learning Vietnamese from them. The lawyer was more serious, he didn't see learning Vietnamese was necessary so he just sat and read his book. My cousins hoped they could catch the engineer and the lawyer's eyes so they can go to American someday, even though both of them had girlfriends. Leaving Vietnam was not an easy task, especially my cousins tried on the wrong men. The engineer and the lawyer were not jokers about relationship even though my cousins were all pretty and attractive. Even me living in America and having no trouble with the language with them, I still didn't have a hope on them because I think they had too much pride on them. I had a crush on the lawyer, but he was so serious and business. He didn't talk as much as the engineer. We tried to be with him, but he observed people more than talking with people. The lawyer wanted to learn Vietnamese only when my cousins asked him to or else he just sat there and observed us like the toys playing with him. Well, my cousins purpose was to close to the engineer and the lawyer as much as they could to have a chance to go to America. The engineer and the lawyer wanted to be with my cousins just like those lively toys for them to play killing times. I didn't know what to say and to feel, but looked at them I considered me as a coward.

After a week in Saigon, we went to Mui Ne beach; I found it was beautiful and lovely to watch the sea wave running in and out when the sun set, and I used to hate to see the sea. We rented a carbin facing the sea shore. The water was cold and the seawave was rolling high that we couldn't swim. The lawyer, the engineer, my little brother, and me went to a swimming pool near by. The engineer taught me how to swim, but my breathing wasn't good enough under the water. I tried so hard to learn and the engineer patiently told me, "It takes time." However, I didn't have a strong feeling for the engineer like I did to the lawyer. I just felt the engineer as a bestfriend. The lawyer reminded me everything about my boyfriend; his voice, his laugh, and his personality. I was joking with the lawyer in the swimming pool. I couldn't pull his pants down, but he almost pulled mine. I took his eyes glasses, but he still could see. I felt the warm from his arm when he held my body like I felt my boyfriend. I just missed my boyfriend so much that I wished the lawyer could replace Benny at that time. I was trembling and thought I was just a fool. The love thought just all over me and I thought like a replicant of my boyfriend. I was crazy since I had the crush on the lawyer. I was afraid to be near him and looked into his eyes. I told myself, "Is it love or a strong feeling came back when I lelf my boyfriend" I just confused and refused that the lawyer was too good for me.

It was raining after three days. We went to Nha Trang beach and it was still raining all day. I was right; raining always gave me a sad feeling. We went to an Aquarium near by watching all kind of fishes. Even though there was a host telling name of each fish, my mind always sufferred from the words, "I wished Benny was here". We not allowed to go to the beach because it was thunder and the sea wave was so high. The lawyer and the engineer wanted to dive under water, but the sea was not calm. My dad met some of his old friends when he was in navy. The lawyer, the engineer, my little brother, and me just walked along the seashore. The lawyer seemed not comfortable with me in the beginning. I think the engineer probably told him about my crush because they were bestfriend. I heard they talked about girls. I felt jealous, but I asked myself "What's for. I wasn't belong to him."

We went back to Saigon after three days. On the way, the back window was broken because the driver bummed into some rocks. I didn't feel good and vomit. The lawyer and the driver fixed it and we made it home alright. The lawyer and the engineer wanted to go diving in Thailand and they went as their plan. I wished they had fun time and alright back to America even though I missed the lawyer. I found down that I couldn't love someone because he reminded me of Benny.

Dad had some business to take care of at Vung Tau beach. My family went there with one of my aunt's family also went along with us. We just watched the seawaves and ate crabs while my dad talked business with his friends. We also stopped by Long Hai beach near Vung Tau. The weather was warm in Long Hai. My little brother and my cousin had a lot of fun swimming at the sea shore. I got hurt so bad by an under rock that I couldn't play with the water. I just took a bath under the sun. We went to Coral shopping and my uncle-in-law hosted us. He was a very fun man and reacted to people very well. I admired his hospitality a lot. I spent money on something that I didn't figure out what was that. My mom whined all the times for she didn't know where all her money had gone. My dad gave her money and she got complained from dad.

My uncle-in-law took my family to "Rex" hotel. It was not just a hotel. We had dinner over there and I loved to watch all those girls in the red long dress perfomed the traditional dance in the north Vietnam.

After the dinner, we went to listen to the music in a night club near by named QueenBy. That night, one of my favorite singer, Thanh Lam was singing. I loved her voice so much and I could feel that I missed someone. It was Benny that I could ever forget. I wished he could feel me like the way I felt him.

On the next day, It was Sunday. My cousins, my little brother and I went to Water Park. One of my cousins was scared of all the rides, she just ran around the lake and floating on the water. My little brother loved all the rides that he went over and over again for ten times each ride. One of my other cousins and me was scared of the rides too, but we still tried each ride one time let see how scared it was. My cousin was a very flirty girl. She flirted around with those security guys in the Water Park. They never let out of her and asked her for a date. There was a cute guy kept looking at me. He came talking to me, but his accent in the middle region made me very hard to understand and he was skinny too. I didn't feel like going out with any Saigon boys in Vietnam. I didn't know; perhaps I still loved Benny a lot.

When I left Vietnam ten years ago, one of my uncle was a happy and enegetic young man. Now he wasn't him anymore. Of course he still smiled and fun to be with, but I could tell there was sadness inside of him and I was right after talking to one of my aunt about his history. I could see in his eyes that he wanted to correct his mistake, but it was too late. His wife and him weren't happy together, they stayed together because of their kids. They chose to be that way because his family stopped him before he was married to his wife, but he was stubbornly against every advices. He took my little brother and I going places to places to eat. I never felt I was closed to him this way ten years ago. Listening to all the words from his heart, I told myself getting it as an experience and don't follow his step. Living without family is lonely, but my uncle would rather be lonely than regret and endure all the pain from his mistake of marrying his wife. I loved Benny, but will it be a mistake when I marry him? When one wanted to marry and the other one didn't want it and if the marriage still happens, it won't be happy and I guaranty that. It just like forcing to live with each other.

On the last three days we were in Vietnam. One of my aunts' family and my family were joined the count down in Caravelle Hotel in Saigon. We enjoyed the dinner and the fashion show in the hotel. After that, my cousins and my uncle in law went to the disco in the hotel. We danced almost all night even though the D.J was not too good. At least we had a very good time. That was all I remembered during the trip back to Vietnam after ten years. I thought I could never see back my motherland because I couldn't afford the trip, but my dad made it happenned. I appreciated him a lot and never regretted to have a dad like him. He was a conservative man, but that the way he was.

Foreword

The tamarind leaves never talked that did not mean they never cried in pain. They expressed their pain their pain by the bitterly taste perhaps. For the first time, I could feel my mom pain when her parent dismissed her out off the house. For the first time, whenever I closed my eyes I saw the shadow of the tamarind trees leaning beside me; the green tamarind leaves were hanging around my body. The full road of green leaves, my heart, my soul since I was a little schoolgirl and filled with dreams. I wished I could see my maternal grandpa again and asked him to tell me the story of the little mermaid. I did not know real love was lament. I wished someone could thrash me until I died so I did not have to think about sadness. I still heard my maternal grandma's acrid voice, "You are a barrier who abandoned by your own parent."